In Search

Cumbria and the Arctic in the
Eighteenth and Nineteenth
Centuries

In Search of Arctic Wonders

Cumbria and the Arctic in the Eighteenth and Nineteenth Centuries

Rob David

CUMBERLAND AND WESTMORLAND
ANTIQUARIAN AND ARCHAEOLOGICAL SOCIETY
2013

Cumberland and Westmorland
Antiquarian and Archaeological Society
Hon. General Editor
Professor Colin Richards

In Search of Arctic Wonders

Cumbria and the Arctic in the Eighteenth and Nineteenth Centuries

EXTRA SERIES NO. XXXIX

© Rob David, 2013. All rights reserved
The moral rights of the author have been asserted

ISBN 978 1 873124 60 4

Printed by
Titus Wilson & Son, Kendal
2013

No part of this publication may be reproduced in any form or stored in a retrieval system or transmitted in any form or by any means electronic, mechanical, photocopying, recording, or otherwise without the prior written permission of the copyright owner or as expressly permitted by law.

Requests for the copyright owner's written permission to reproduce any part of this publication should be made of the copyright owner through the CWAAS.

Contents

LIST OF FIGURES	VII
ACKNOWLEDGEMENTS	XI
FOREWORD	XIII
CHAPTER 1 'They forged the last link with their lives': Introduction: The British in the Arctic	1
CHAPTER 2 'A Voyage of Discovery towards the North Pole': Skeffington Lutwidge in 1773	9
CHAPTER 3 'For sale: a quantity of whale oil': Whaling from Whitehaven 1762-1791	33
CHAPTER 4 'Ships that have left their bones in the battlefield of Melville Bay': The Arctic voyages of *Alfred* and *Jumna*, 1809 – 1863	47
CHAPTER 5 'I know it is in existence, and not very hard to find': Searching for the North West Passage, 1818-1859	63
CHAPTER 6 'I am told I am going to an Unhabited land': The Yellow Earl in the Arctic, 1888-9	87
CHAPTER 7 'An intellectual entertainment for intellectual people': The Rural Imagination and the Arctic	101
APPENDICES	
APPENDIX 1 Places to visit in Cumbria	121
APPENDIX 2 'Sir John Franklin's ill-fated expedition: The lament of the last man, on his way to the Great Fish River' by Beilby Porteus	128
GLOSSARY	131

List of Figures

1.1. Map of the Arctic region
1.2. Pack ice in the Greenland Sea
1.3. Summer in Melville Bay, north-west Greenland
1.4. Map of the geographical features associated with the search for the North West Passage
2.1. Portrait of Skeffington Lutwidge by Gilbert Stuart (painted c1783-84)
2.2. Letter of 2 June 1763 from Skeffington Lutwidge to the Navy Board in London
2.3. 'A profile and section of the additional works fitted on board His Majesty's Sloop the *Carcass* at Sheerness in April 1773'
2.4. 'Plan of Upp. Deck and fore and after platform of the *Carcass* Sloop taken off at Sheerness April 1773'
2.5. Navy Board: Navy Pay Office: Ship's Pay Books. Ship: *Carcass*
2.6. Chart showing the track of His Majesty's Sloops *Racehorse* and *Carcass*
2.7. A page from Skeffington Lutwidge's journal including the entry for 5 July 1773
2.8. A Spitsbergen beach covered in driftwood
2.9. View of the *Racehorse* and *Carcass*, 7 August 1773: based on the engraving by John Cleveley, *Hauling boats over the ice off Spitsbergen, August 7th, 1773*
2.10. 'Nelson and the Bear' by Richard Westall, c1806
2.11. The front elevation of Holmrook Hall in the early 1940s
2.12. The surviving gate to the stable yard at Holmrook Hall
2.13. The gardener's cottage and the walled garden at Holmrook Hall
2.14. Irton church
2.15. Part of the memorial to Admiral Skeffington Lutwidge erected by his nephew Major Skeffington Lutwidge at Irton Church
3.1. Extract from Muster Roll for *Golden Lion* sailing from Liverpool, 1778
3.2. *Neptune* whaling in the East Greenland Sea 1778
3.3. *Neptune* nipped by ice in the East Greenland Sea 1778
3.4. Summary of the whaling activity of Whitehaven-built ships, 1762-1791
3.5. Daniel Brocklebank's residence in Roper Street, Whitehaven
3.6. Advertisement in the *Cumberland Pacquet* for the sale of whale oil, September 1787
3.7. The beach at Parton
4.1. Whitehaven harbour 1816
4.2. Muster Roll for *Alfred* sailing from Lancaster to Martinico 1801-2

4.3. List of whaling vessels sailing from Hull to the Northern Whale Fishery in 1821
4.4. The purchases by crew members of *Alfred* as recorded in the Hay and Company ledger, 1847
4.5. Whitehaven harbour from Bransty Hill c1830
5.1. Portrait of Sir John Barrow by George Thomas Payne, after John Lucas, published 27 May 1847
5.2. The house at Dragley Beck, Ulverston, where John Barrow was born
5.3. The Hoad Monument, Ulverston
5.4. The Sir John Barrow memorial plaque inside the Hoad Monument
5.5. The *Illustrated London News* report of the laying of the foundation stone of the memorial to Sir John Barrow, 25 May 1850
5.6. Portrait of Sir John Richardson by Stephen Pearce, 1850
5.7. Lancrigg, Grasmere, Sir John Richardson's home 1855-1865
5.8. The memorial to Sir John Richardson in St Oswald's Church, Grasmere
5.9. The painting of Captain William Edward Parry at Tower Hill, Crosthwaite
5.10. Portrait of Captain William Edward Parry painted by Samuel Drummond, 1820
5.11. Engraving of Captain William Edward Parry, by J. Thomson, 1 March, 1821, for the *European Magazine and London Review*
5.12. The name 'Parry' carved on the rock slab at Ecclerigg Quarry, Windermere
5.13. The name 'Ross' carved on the rock slab at Ecclerigg Quarry, Windermere
5.14. Portrait of Captain John Ross by James Green, 1833
5.15. Captain James Clark Ross by R. M. Hodgetts, after John Robert Wildman, published 1835
5.16. Engraving 'McClintock's travelling party discovering remains of cairn at Cape Herschel', in F.L McClintock, *The Voyage of the 'Fox' in the Arctic Seas: A Narrative of the Discovery of the Fate of Sir John Franklin and his Companions*, 1859
5.17. The plaque inside the Hoad Monument listing the 'Monument Keepers' including 'William Jones, late Arctic Yacht "Fox" 1860-1862'
6.1. Photograph of the Earl of Lonsdale in clothing he brought back from the Arctic taken in April 1889.
6.2. Lowther Castle in 1910 showing the Earl's fleet of yellow cars
6.3. Photograph of Violet Cameron (1855-1910) probably taken during the 1880s
6.4. Map of the Earl of Lonsdale's journey through the Canadian Arctic and Alaska, 1888-89

LIST OF FIGURES ix

6.5. Eskimo-Aleut Harpoon-head and line made of steel, ivory, cord, horn and hide(?)
6.6. Gauntlets made of skin (fish, salmon?), grass and hide: South-West Alaska Eskimos
6.7. A Pacific Eskimo mask made of wood, feathers and quills, probably collected in Alaska
6.8. Model Umiak or boat with five figures (a women's boat) made of skin, wood, wool and down, probably purchased in Alaska
7.1. The poster for Rignold's *Panorama of the Arctic Regions* which was shown at Shrewsbury, 16 October 1876.
7.2. The whalebone arch near Burneside in the early twentieth century
7.3. Extracts from the catalogue of Peter Crosthwaite's museum, Keswick
7.4. Extract from the Catalogue of Museum of the Kendal Literary and Scientific Society, 1870
7.5. Part of the first of two instalments describing 'Lord Lonsdale's Travels in Arctic North America' that appeared in the *Illustrated London News*, 4 January, 1890
7.6. An engraving of Greta Hall and Keswick Bridge by W. Westall/E. Francis
7.7. An engraving 'Fort Norman on the Mackenzie River' based on a Lonsdale photograph, *Illustrated London News*, 4. January, 1890
7.8. A photograph of the Earl of Lonsdale in Arctic attire taken by I. W. Taber in San Francisco during his return journey in 1889
7.9. The engraving created from the photograph in Figure 7.8 which was published in the *Illustrated London News*, 11 January 1890
7.10. 'A Noonday Halt. Temperature 55 Degrees below Zero', *Illustrated London News*, 11 January 1890
7.11. 'York Factory, West Coast of Hudson's Bay', *Illustrated London News*, 4 January 1890
7.12. Part of the sale catalogue for the contents of Lowther Castle, 1947
7.13. The polar bear killed by the Yellow Earl which was placed in the entrance hall of Lowther Castle
A1. Map of the main places to visit in Cumbria
A2. The remains of the whalebone arch near Burneside
A3. The remains of the entrance to Holmrook Hall
A4. Estate buildings at Holmrook Hall
A5. Greta Hall, Keswick
A6. The ruins of Lowther Castle
A7. The grave of the Yellow Earl and his wife Cicelie at Lowther Church
A8. A general photograph of one of the inscribed slabs at Cragwood
A9. Photograph of Beilby Porteus

Acknowledgements

I am grateful to the following for answering questions when I asked for help: John Borron, David Bradbury, Mike Lea, Diana Matthews, Michele Moatt, Denis Perriam, Henry Summerson, Les Tallon, Barbara Todd and David Weston. John Borron, Sue David, and Mike and Kate Lea read parts of earlier drafts of the manuscript and provided numerous suggestions for improvement. Anne Savours kindly read the whole manuscript and this book has benefited enormously from her knowledge of the subject. Colin Richards, the General Editor of the Cumberland and Westmorland Antiquarian and Archaeological Society, has steered this volume through the publishing process. Within Cumbria I have made extensive use of the four offices of the Cumbria Archive Service, the Local Studies libraries at Carlisle, Kendal and Whitehaven, the Armitt Museum and Library at Ambleside, and Keswick Museum and Art Gallery. Maggie and Julian Sale, Mike Lea and Tess Pike kindly took some of the photographs. As always the archivists, librarians and curators have been unstinting of their time and expertise. Bryan Harper drew the maps.

The author is grateful to the following people and organisations for permission to publish illustrations:
Captain Cook Memorial Museum, Whitby: 2.6
Chrysler Museum of Art, Norfolk, Virginia: 2.1
Church Wardens, PCC and Vicar of St Cuthbert's Church, Edenhall: A9
Cumbria County Council, Carlisle Library: 2.11, 4.1, 4.5, 6.2, 7.2, 7.6, 7.12
Cumbria County Council, Kendal Library: 7.3, 7.4
Hull Maritime Museums: Hull Museums: 4.3
John Holmes: 5.9
John Spedding, Mirehouse: 3.2, 3.3
Kendal College, Kendal: 7.13
Lowther Estate Trust: 6.1, 7.8
National Archives, London: 2.2, 2.5, 2.7, 3.1, 4.2
National Maritime Museum, Greenwich, London: 2.3, 2.4, 2.9, 2.10
National Portrait Gallery, London: 5.1, 5.6, 5.10, 5.14, 5.15
Shetland Archives: 4.4
Shropshire Archives: 7.1
Theatre Museum, Victoria and Albert Museum, London: 6.3
Trustees of the British Museum, London: 6.5, 6.6, 6.7, 6.8

The author and publishers have taken all reasonable steps to obtain permission for all the images in this book, but apologise for any omissions or errors when owners could not be traced or have been incorrectly identified.

This book has benefited from financial support provided by the Cumberland and Westmorland Antiquarian and Archaeological Society Research and Grants Committee, and the Trustees of the Curwen and Kirby Archive Trusts.

Some of the material in chapters 3, 4, 5 and 6 has appeared in articles published in *Transactions of the Cumberland and Westmorland Antiquarian and Archaeological Society* and in *Northern History*. The discussion in Chapter 7 is based upon a paper delivered to 'Polar Visual Culture: An International Conference' at the University of St Andrews in June 2011.

Foreword

When the Fifth Earl of Lonsdale, the 'Yellow Earl', re-emerged in San Francisco from his journey across northern Canada and Alaska in April 1889, the press was on hand to report on the many 'Arctic wonders' he encountered. A born story-teller, he gave the newspapers exactly what they wanted. The headlines screamed: 'One of the Greatest on Record…..A Wonderful Series of Adventures….. The Explorer Reaches 75 Degrees North…..Amid Great Privations……Savage and Gigantic Esquimaux Discovered'. In the Yellow Earl's case the reality, although still exciting, was not quite so colourful. He was not so much the last explorer as one of the first traveller-tourists in search of adventure, and so placed Cumbria and Cumbrians in the vanguard of developments that positioned the Arctic as a recreational destination.

Just over a century earlier, in 1773, another Cumbrian, Skeffington Lutwidge, had tried to pioneer a route through what was thought to be a barrier of ice encircling open water, the so-called 'Open Polar Sea' at the North Pole, in the hope of reaching the riches of China and the East. In his day the quests for economic advantage and for scientific understanding were key motivators for those who organised expeditions to the Arctic.

For just over half a century between 1818 and 1859, Britain led the way in searching for a route through the maze of islands and passages north of the Canadian mainland to the Pacific – the North West Passage. Economic motivation quickly gave way to desire for national and, sometimes, personal glory, and to the search for geographical knowledge and scientific understanding. The person who inspired this programme of discovery was another Cumbrian – Sir John Barrow – and some of those he sent to the Arctic came to have their own connections to Cumbria and to Cumbrians.

While explorers hit the headlines, whalers with far less publicity went about their business of catching whales in the Arctic seas to provide materials essential for industry and domestic living. Whitehaven was part of this industry - building whale ships, acting as a minor centre of the whaling trade and providing crews for whalers based at other ports.

Cumbria was part of the national story of Arctic exploration and exploitation during the eighteenth and nineteenth centuries. This book considers how Cumbrians from a variety of backgrounds participated in this colourful episode in the nation's history. This era of heroic exploration was significant as it was a period which saw an enormous increase in geographical knowledge and understanding of the Arctic regions alongside the shattering of some illusions, and which concluded with the emergence of the polar world of the north as an adventure destination. This book also makes a contribution to recent discussions about how those who did not have opportunities to visit the region learnt about the exotic world that was being discovered, and what they were being told. Although it cannot be claimed that Cumbrians were involved with every facet of the opening up of the Arctic during the eighteenth and nineteenth centuries, nor that those who stayed at home had access to all the representations available to people living in cities, this book shows that Cumbria was less isolated and inward-looking than often portrayed.

The subject matter of this book inevitably draws upon the specialist language of explorers, mariners, geographers and scientists of the time. A glossary of the terms they used can be found on pages 131-133.

A NOTE ON THE USE OF GEOGRAPHICAL AND CULTURAL NAMES

At the time of the events described in this book the county of Cumbria did not exist. The post-1974 county incorporates the old counties of Cumberland and Westmorland along with Furness (or Lancashire-over-Sands) and those parts of the West Riding of Yorkshire around Sedbergh and Dent. References to Cumbria and Cumbrians in this book relate to all these places and their inhabitants.

As the subject matter relates to the eighteenth and nineteenth centuries, the Arctic place names of that era are used rather than the names now being used by the indigenous populations. On the other hand the now little-used word 'eskimo' has been replaced by the words 'Inuit' and 'Greenlander' for the inhabitants of Arctic Canada and Greenland respectively, except in quotations from the period.

Chapter 1
'They forged the last link with their lives':
Introduction: The British in the Arctic

During the sixteenth century merchants and mariners, mainly from England, became interested in the Arctic. At that time the north held a particular fascination as Peter Davidson has sought to explain:

> An important part of the perception of the north, and the crucial reason for undertaking the most dangerous of northern voyages, is that it is a place of treasures and marvels. Not only is the north the site of prodigies – icebergs, volcanoes, the magnetic mountain – it is also the place from which come the treasures – furs, ivory, and amber, which are the luxuries of the south.

Commerce and science, as well as, for some, personal glory were important incentives for polar exploration but in time the demands of national prestige undermined a more rational purpose.

It was during the sixteenth century that it became obvious that the American continent formed a formidable barrier to trade with the Orient. The tortuous Strait of Magellan to the south was not an effective route for commerce, and in order to find a route that could provide an alternative to the long voyage around the Cape of Good Hope and across the Indian Ocean, traders became interested in the potential of a route to the East around the north of North America – the North West Passage, and around the north of the Eurasian landmass – the North East Passage. Despite the interests of the Muscovy Company in an eastern route, it was the western route that saw more activity, especially by the English. It was hoped that there might be a sea route through the North American landmass, but by the end of the sixteenth century the French discovered that the St Lawrence River did not provide a route to the East, and during the seventeenth century British voyagers searching even further north learnt that there was no way through Hudson Bay nor any obvious route westward through Davis Strait and Baffin Bay. The extent of the exploration of the north by mariners from the British Isles is shown through the place names on modern atlases (Figure 1.1). Promoters, or projectors as they were often known, and adventurers appropriated the seas and coasts, already well known to the Inuit, by naming

Figure 1.1. Map of the Arctic region.

them after themselves. The memory of Henry Hudson (Hudson Bay and Hudson Strait), John Davis (Davis Strait), William Baffin (Baffin Bay and Baffin Island), Martin Frobisher (Frobisher Bay), Luke Foxe (Foxe Basin) and Thomas James (James Bay) has survived to recent times in names on maps (Figure 1.4), although more recently the strengthening of an Inuit cultural identity in northern Canada and Greenland has led to settlements and some geographical names being renamed in their native languages.*

* For example political entities such as Nunavut replace a large part of the old North West Territories in Canada, and Greenlanders now refer to Greenland as Kalaallit Nunaat. The community of Frobisher Bay on Baffin Island is now known as Iqaluit, and the capital of Greenland, Godhaab, has been renamed Nuuk. Scoresbysund, the most northerly village on the east coast of Greenland and named after the British whaling captain and explorer, William Scoresby, is now known as Ittoqqortoormiit, and the adjacent fjord of the same name has been renamed Kangertittivaq.

During the eighteenth century commercial opportunities in the Arctic were increasingly exploited. In northern Canada trading companies, pre-eminent amongst which was the Hudson's Bay Company founded by royal charter in 1670, established forts and trading posts across much of the northern territories. Furs and skins were much sought after in Europe and the American colonies (later the United States), and the company employees worked alongside native peoples to bring the products of the north to the markets of the south. Some employees of these trading companies, such as Samuel Hearne of the Hudson's Bay Company and Sir Alexander Mackenzie of the North West Company, combined company work with the exploration of northern Canada.

At the same time Arctic whaling was being developed, initially by the Dutch in the Spitsbergen fishery, but later by the British in the East Greenland Sea and in Baffin Bay and Davis Strait (the Northern Whale Fishery). The whale of choice was the Bowhead or Greenland Right whale *(Balaena mysticetus)*, a large mammal up to 20 metres long and weighing up to 120 tons, which very conveniently, so far as the whale-hunters were concerned, floated when dead. British industry had multiple uses for whale products. A huge quantity of whale oil was needed by the expanding woollen industry, where it was used to clean wool for spinning and in the manufacture of coarse cloth such as military cloth. Whale oil was also used as a lubricant for machinery in mills and mines, and it constituted an ingredient in varnish, paint and putty, increasing quantities of which were required by the building trade at a time of urban expansion. Streets were lit, where they were lit at all, with whale oil. Oil lamps were used to keep the mills open at night, and in the home spermaceti candles (using oil from the sperm whale) were considered superior to tallow ones. Spermaceti oil was also used as a lubricant in clocks and watches. In addition baleen (whale bone) had multiple domestic uses, for example as umbrella spokes, in door locks and brooms and in the manufacture of corsets. When crushed it could be used as a manure. New uses for whale products were under investigation. According to the *Westmorland Gazette* in 1835 'whale oil has been proved equal to bones in raising turnip'. Whitehaven became involved in this trade by sending ships to the Arctic, processing the products of whales, and building vessels that became whale ships at other United Kingdom ports (see Chapters 3 and 4). Most of the vessels sank, 'nipped' by the shifting pack ice, often in the particularly dangerous waters of Melville Bay in north-west Greenland (Figures 1.2 and 1.3). However, during the eighteenth century, as Glyn Williams has pointed out, 'the commercial advantages of a short sea-route to the East remained as compelling as ever – it would cut a twelve-month voyage to six weeks, one optimist estimated – and evidence was shaped to fit the thesis'. Projectors and publicists promoted numerous voyages that attempted to find a way westward from Hudson Bay, and every sound on its west coast, such as Chesterfield Inlet, Wager Bay and

Repulse Bay was explored, but without success.

It was thought that another route to the East was possible through what was expected to be an ice-free polar sea which would be found beyond the ice barrier north of Spitsbergen. In 1773 the Admiralty sent Constantine Phipps and Skeffington Lutwidge, who was born in Whitehaven and later lived at Holmrook near Gosforth on the west coast of Cumbria (see Chapter 2), on a voyage to find a route into the 'Open Polar Sea' which, it was hoped, would lead them relatively easily to the East and provide significant opportunities for scientific observations. Inevitably the voyage failed in the geographical objective, but it was very successful scientifically. In Phipps's account of the voyage, the appendices set the standard for future scientific work in the Arctic. They included sections on navigation, meteorology, natural history, astronomy and even desalination. The two ships returned to Britain during the autumn of that year.

The Admiralty sent more elaborate voyages under the command of James Cook and George Vancouver into the Pacific Ocean to explore the west coast of North America, and in 1778 Cook entered the Arctic Ocean through the Bering Strait. The short summer season ensured that he was unable to explore beyond Icy Cape on the northern coast of Alaska before being forced back by the moving pack ice. Cook summed up the difficulties explorers faced in this Arctic zone in a letter of October 1778 written to the Admiralty: 'We were upon a Coast where every step was to be considered, where no information could be had from Maps, either modern or ancient: confiding too much in the former we were frequently misled to our no small hindrance'.

Glyn Williams has explained the delusion that caused Great Britain and the Admiralty to devote excessive resources to the elusive North West Passage in the eighteenth century: 'Rather like generals in some endless war of attrition, those projectors who sent expeditions to find the Northwest Passage were always convinced that the next "push" would pass through all obstacles to achieve its objective'.

The French wars at the end of the eighteenth century halted exploration, but in 1818 Great Britain once again embarked on a quest to find the North West Passage. By this time few people believed that its discovery could have a commercial benefit, but many felt that its continued exploration and the discovery of a route were challenges that, given the country's past commitment, should be achieved by the nation. National prestige supported by scientific discovery now became the prime objectives, and as in the previous century, many felt that a failure should be followed by another offensive, and that a 'final push' would achieve success.

The prime mover behind this surge of activity in the Arctic was Sir John Barrow, the Second Secretary of the Admiralty for almost the whole of the period 1804 – 1845. John Barrow (see Chapter 5) was born in Ulverston in Cumbria, and although he had little to do with the town as an adult, his great memorial, the Hoad Monument, was built there after he died. Barrow sent many expeditions to explore the straits and islands to the north of the Canadian mainland, and to travel down the river valleys of northern Canada to the shores of the Arctic Ocean to map the vast area of unknown territory. Some of the voyages and explorations of John Franklin, Edward Parry, John Ross, James Clark Ross, Frederick Beechey, John Rae, George Back and John Richardson were made possible by Barrow's promotion of Arctic exploration. Although the priority was the discovery of a route to the East, science was not neglected. Parry provided detailed information about the Inuit people he encountered, Richardson focused on reporting on natural history and medicine, and James Clark Ross concentrated on astronomy and magnetism, including discovering the location of the North Magnetic Pole on the Boothia Peninsula on 2 June 1831. The names of Parry, and one of the two Rosses (it is unclear which one), are so high profile that they appear in Cumbria in unexpected surroundings. Sir John Richardson retired to Grasmere and was

Figure 1.2. Pack ice in the Greenland Sea *(photograph: Rob David)*

buried there. These explorers and their links to Cumbria are also discussed in Chapter 5.

The disappearance of Franklin, his two vessels HMS *Terror* and HMS *Erebus* and the 134 officers and men placed under his command, while searching for the North West Passage in 1845, led to many searching expeditions and further exploration of the Arctic coast by expeditions commissioned by the Admiralty, by Franklin's wife Jane and by private individuals. In the process the geography of northern Canada was revealed. A parliamentary committee awarded a prize for the discovery of the North West Passage to the officers and crew of *Investigator* (Captain Robert McClure) although the traverse was only completed by abandoning their ship, sledging across the pack ice, and returning home in *Resolute* which had been sent to look out for them. Other North West Passage routes were identified by John Rae and Richard Collinson, and the ultimate fate of Franklin and his ships' companies was explained by John Rae and Leopold McClintock. Rae returned to Britain in 1854 with a collection of artefacts which had been acquired by local Inuit from the two ships and the bodies of the dead sailors, and produced a report based on Inuit accounts that read: 'From the mutilated state of many of the corpses, and the contents of the kettles, it is evident that our wretched countrymen had been driven to the last resource – cannibalism – as a means of prolonging existence'. In 1859 McClintock returned with further relics of Franklin's expedition and a document recovered from a stone cairn outlining events from 1845 to 1848. This recorded the decision to abandon the ships by those who still survived in April 1848, with the intention, not realised, of making their way to the south over the ice to the river systems of northern Canada.

Lady Jane Franklin's determination to immortalise her husband and his companions was successfully achieved with the erection of the monument in Waterloo Place in London in 1866 on which was written Sir John Richardson's motto, 'They forged the last link with their lives'. In the words of his recent biographer, Andrew Lambert, this 'turned Franklin and his men

Figure 1.3. A summer view of part of Melville Bay in north-west Greenland where many whaling vessels were 'nipped' by the ice and sank *(photograph: Rob David)*

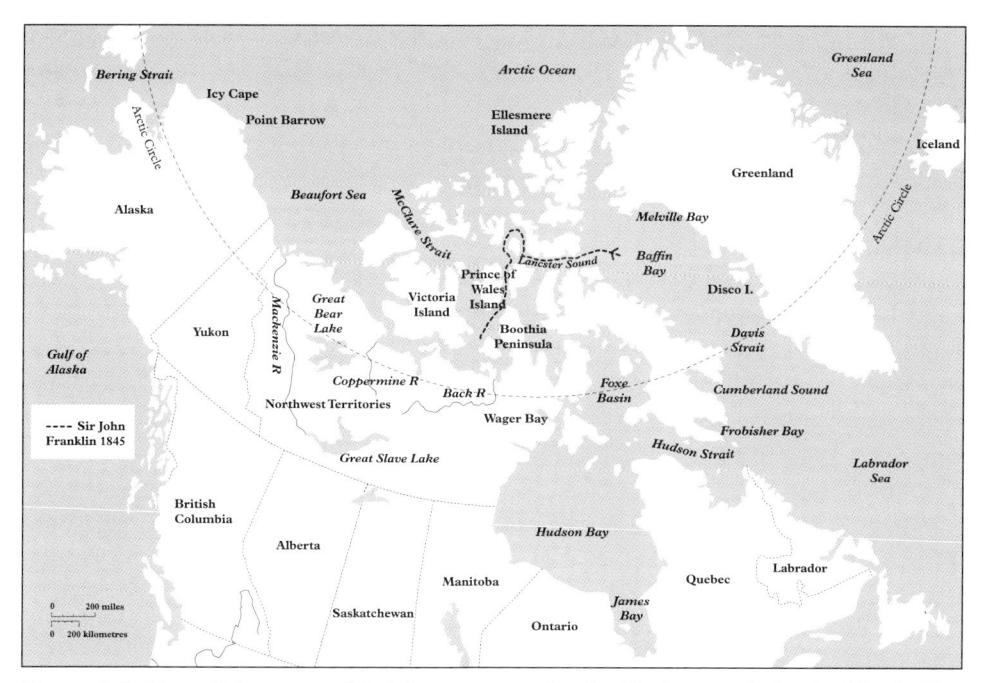

Figure 1.4. Map of the geographical features associated with the search for the North West Passage.

into paragons of the mid-Victorian cult of service, heroes who had willingly sacrificed their lives for the greater good, [by obscuring] the catastrophic failure of the expedition'. Despite Lady Jane, horror at the fate of Franklin and his men made Victorian society question the value of sending British officers and crew on Arctic journeys when the benefit was so uncertain. Between 1859 and 1875 the Admiralty withdrew from Arctic exploration, and there were few privately-funded voyages. In 1875 the Admiralty sent George Nares to find a route over the ice to the North Pole (the idea of an open polar sea had long been abandoned except by a few diehards). The death by scurvy of some members of the expedition did nothing to improve the image of Arctic exploration, and as the nineteenth century came to an end, British interest in polar exploration was increasingly transferred to the Antarctic. It was left to Norway and Roald Amundsen to sail the North West Passage and to the United States and Robert Peary (although his claim has not gone unchallenged) to reach the North Pole. For Britain the Arctic became the destination of the wealthy traveller whose aim was to hunt the creatures of the north and return with preserved skins and stuffed animals to add to their 'trophy' back home. One of these was Hugh Lowther, the fifth Earl of Lonsdale, who took the opportunity while escaping from some unwelcome publicity at home to add polar bears, musk oxen and other arctic fauna to his trophy at Lowther Castle in Cumbria. His extraordinary journey with its varied outcomes is explored in Chapter 6.

Although few people beyond explorers, whalers and the occasional wealthy traveller had opportunities to visit the Arctic, its characteristics became increasingly widely known during the eighteenth and nineteenth centuries. Neighbours, friends and families of those who had visited the Arctic no doubt learnt at second-hand about the region. Many explorers wrote accounts of their travels, and the national and regional press, as well as the weekly illustrated magazines that became so popular during the nineteenth century, kept the public informed of the progress of expeditions even if the news they were reporting was sometimes years out of date. Both books and newspapers included engravings (and later photographs) of the activities of the explorers, the scenery and the native peoples of the Arctic. With the emergence of a network of public libraries, people of all classes increasingly had access to these accounts and images. Elsewhere the Arctic was illustrated, with varying degrees of fancifulness, by artists, illustrators of children's books, creators of panoramas and manufacturers of plates, tins and other household artefacts whose surfaces could be decorated with topical scenes. Occasionally native peoples from the Canadian Arctic and from Greenland were brought back to Britain and placed on display for their educational and entertainment value. Cumbrians had access to many of these representations of the north, and the images and imaginings that these engendered are discussed in Chapter 7.

★ ★ ★ ★ ★

SUGGESTED FURTHER READING

E. C. Coleman, *The Royal Navy in Polar Exploration from Frobisher to Ross*, (Stroud, Tempus, 2006).

P. Davidson, *The Idea of the North*, (London, Reaktion Books, 2005).

J. P. Delgado, *Across the Top of the World: The Quest for the Northwest Passage*, (London, British Museum Press, 1999).

G. Jackson, *The British Whaling Trade*, (London, A & C Black, 1978; [reprinted in *Research in Maritime History*, No.29, 2005]).

A. Lambert, *Franklin: Tragic Hero of Polar Navigation*, (London, Faber and Faber, 2009).

A. Savours, *The Search for the North West Passage*, (London, Chatham, 1999).

R. Vaughan, *The Arctic: A History*, (Stroud, Alan Sutton, 1994).

G. Williams, *Voyages of Delusion: The Northwest Passage in the Age of Reason*, (London, HarperCollins, 2002).

G. Williams, *Arctic Labyrinth: The Quest for the Northwest Passage*, (London, Allen Lane, 2009).

Chapter 2
'A Voyage of Discovery towards the North Pole': Skeffington Lutwidge in 1773

In the spring of 1773 Captain Skeffington Lutwidge (Figure 2.1), the master and commander of HMS *Carcass*, at that time deployed in the Irish Sea, received an order from the Admiralty to sail to Sheerness in Kent. *Carcass* arrived there on 25 March, 1773. Some three weeks later, on 16 April, Lutwidge was informed that he was to undertake 'a voyage of discovery towards the North Pole', and that *Carcass* 'was to be victualled for Six Months with all Species of provisions…and [he was] to use the utmost dispatch in getting her fitted accordingly'. A ship's company of ninety was to be carefully chosen as 'none but effective men shall serve'. He also learnt that when the ship was ready he was to serve under Captain the Hon. Constantine John Phipps, the commander of *Racehorse*, and should join him at the Nore.

Figure 2.1. Portrait of Skeffington Lutwidge by Gilbert Stuart (painted c1783-84) *(by courtesy of Chrysler Museum of Art, Norfolk, Virginia)*

Skeffington Lutwidge (1737 – 1814) was the tenth and youngest child of Thomas Lutwidge (1670-1745) and his second wife Lucy (died 1780). Thomas Lutwidge had left Dublin about 1690 and settled in Whitehaven where he became a shipowner and merchant with interests in tobacco, malting, brewing and distilling. In 1721, already a widower but without an heir, he married Lucy Hoghton, the youngest child of Sir Henry Hoghton, 5th Baronet of Hoghton Tower in Lancashire and sometime Member of Parliament for that county, and Mary Skeffington, eldest daughter of John Skeffington, Viscount Massereene. By the time Skeffington Lutwidge was born in 1737, Thomas was in financial difficulty due to the loss in 1735 of his partly uninsured ship *Prince Frederick*, which precipitated a cash flow crisis from which he was never able to recover. His inability to repay some substantial debts caused his business to fail around 1741 and he fled his creditors back to Ireland, where he died in 1745.

In his will, Thomas left Lucy his entire estate, which was probably not as valuable as it once had been. It would seem that Lucy and the younger children continued to live in Whitehaven, but nothing is known of Skeffington's upbringing during this time. As the youngest child he needed a career, which was destined to be in the Royal Navy. He was commissioned as a lieutenant in August 1759 at the age of 22, and in 1763 took command of the cutter HMS *Cholmondely*. He remained with her until 1766 serving in the Irish Sea between Liverpool, the Isle of Man and Whitehaven. On occasions he wrote to the Admiralty from Whitehaven asking permission to purchase stores and equipment. On 2 June 1763 he asked whether he could purchase boatswains and carpenters stores, and was authorised only to purchase what was 'absolutely necessary at Whitehaven' (Figure 2.2). On 14 November 1763 he purchased a mast to make a bowsprit while at Whitehaven and sent the bill to London. In June 1771 Lutwidge was back in the Irish Sea commanding HMS *Carcass*.

That Lutwidge found himself second-in-command to Captain Phipps was probably a product of chance. Despite James Cook's recent successful use of Whitby colliers in polar waters, the Admiralty chose two 'Bombs' H.M.Sloop *Carcass* and H.M.Sloop *Racehorse* to go north. Bombs were specially designed to mount heavy mortars (bombs) and required a solid bed on which the weapon could be seated. With the mortar removed and the bows strengthened with extra timbers the vessels were thought to be able to withstand the dangers of moving ice (Figures 2.3 and 2.4). There was also no expertise amongst Royal Navy officers on which the Admiralty could draw. The Admiralty had not sent any ships into Arctic waters since 1741-42 when Christopher Middleton and William Moor had searched for the North West Passage in the area of Wager Bay to the north of Hudson Bay. Since then Arctic navigation had been confined to explorations undertaken by the

Gentlemen

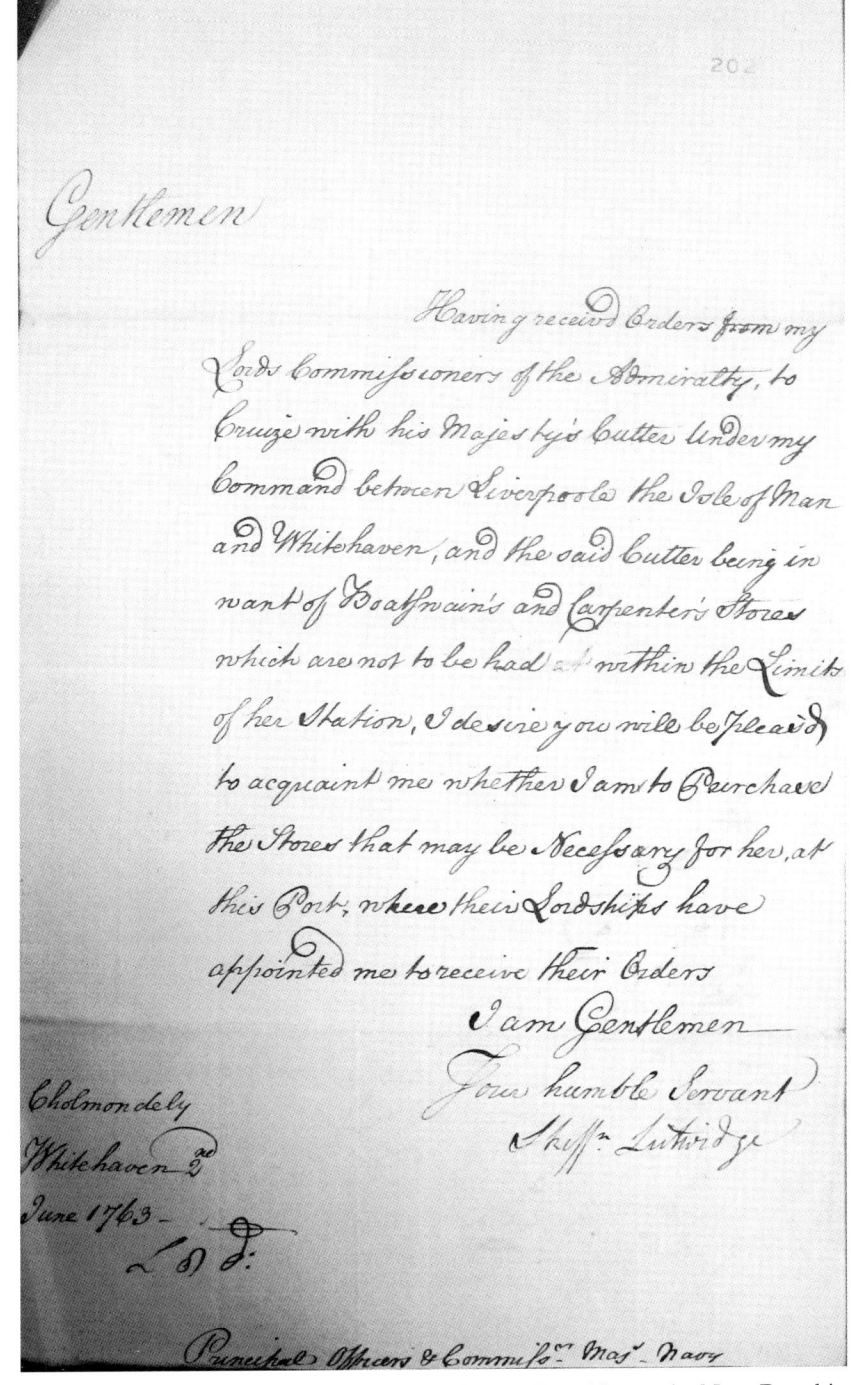

Having received Orders from my Lords Commissioners of the Admiralty, to Cruize with his Majesty's Cutter under my Command between Liverpoole the Isle of Man and Whitehaven, and the said Cutter being in want of Boatswain's and Carpenter's Stores which are not to be had within the Limits of her Station, I desire you will be pleas'd to acquaint me whether I am to Purchase the Stores that may be Necessary for her, at this Port, where their Lordships have appointed me to receive their Orders

I am Gentlemen
Your humble Servant
Skeff.n Lutwidge

Cholmondely
Whitehaven 2.d
June 1763

Principal Officers & Commiss.rs Mas.rs Navy

Figure 2.2. Letter of 2 June 1763 from Skeffington Lutwidge to the Navy Board in London. TNA: ADM106/1124/202: Navy Board: Records. In-letters. Miscellaneous *(reproduced by courtesy of the National Archives, London)*

Hudson's Bay Company, one or two privately financed voyages, and the activities of the whaling fleet in the Greenland Sea around Spitsbergen. As Lutwidge was the existing commander of *Carcass*, the ideal vessel for this voyage, he was, by default, appointed as second-in-command of this expedition.

The purpose of the North Pole expedition of 1773

In the 1770s many believed in an unfrozen or open polar sea, based on the false premises that the salinity of the open sea would mean that there was less ice than near land, and that the continuous daylight of the Arctic summer would cause the melting of ice around the North Pole. This idea had become well established as a result of the work of geographers such as the Dutchman Petrus Plancius (1552-1622), the Russian Mikhail Lomonosov (1711-1765) and the Swiss Samuel Engel (1702 – 1784), as well as the French explorer Louis-Antoine Bougainville (1729-1811). Lomonosov's belief had resulted in two failed Russian attempts to sail to the centre of the Arctic Ocean in 1765 and 1766. On both occasions the ships had been stopped by impenetrable ice just north of Spitsbergen. An enlarged edition of Engel's first book in which he referred to 'a vast open sea' was published in 1772 and was brought to the attention of the Admiralty. This no doubt helped Daines Barrington, a British naturalist-lawyer, gain support for his proposal to the Royal Society in 1773 that Britain should search for just such a route through that 'open sea'. His suggestion was probably influenced by whaling masters returning to Britain claiming that favourable ice conditions had allowed them to reach exceptionally high latitudes north of Spitsbergen. In proposing an expedition he argued that it would be to Britain's commercial advantage as it would enable the opening of a new trade route with the Far East. Secretary of the Royal Society, Dr. Matthew Maty, supported the idea of such a voyage which would also provide opportunities for scientific research and wrote to the First Lord of the Admiralty, Lord Sandwich, that it would be 'of service to the promotion of natural knowledge, the proper object of their [the Society's] institution'. The idea was supported by both organisations largely as a result of the successful blend of science and exploration during James Cook's first circumnavigation of the globe from which he had returned in 1771. Consequently the Admiralty appointed Captain Phipps to 'try how far navigation was possible towards the North Pole'.

The objectives of the Admiralty and the Royal Society did not fit together comfortably. The tone of the Admiralty's *Instructions* to Phipps makes it clear that for them, the geographical objective of reaching the North Pole, along with the strategic and commercial benefits such a voyage might bring, were paramount. On the other hand, the Royal Society was more interested in the new scientific knowledge that could accrue. Phipps was well educated, a fellow of the Royal Society and a friend of Joseph Banks, the scientist on board *Endeavour* who had returned in triumph with Cook in 1771. Phipps was clearly attracted by the scientific opportunities. That this was the case is shown by the fact that more of his published narrative of the voyage, *A Voyage Towards the North Pole undertaken by His Majesty's command 1773*, was concerned with reporting the scientific results than with the events of the voyage itself. However, Skeffington Lutwidge does not seem to have shared that interest as his manuscript journal makes little reference to scientific investigation, and there is scant evidence that he took part in any of the recording that contributed to the scientific appendices in Phipps's book.

According to Thomas Floyd, a midshipman in *Racehorse*, many amongst the ship's company had little concept of where they were going or what the purpose of the voyage was. He wrote in his narrative:

> Many were the conceptions they had formed of the intention, and destination, of our voyage; some (perhaps out of humour, or more likely out of ignorance) said we were going to the North Pole to "cut a piece of it to make a walking stick for the Prince of Wales!"; others "that the Pole wanted scraping and greasing" [resulting from the belief] in an axis on which the globe turned.

Of those who understood the purpose of the voyage it is clear that the geographical objective of entering the open polar sea seems to have been seen as the priority. This is suggested by the anonymous author of the account of the voyage published in 1774 in Volume 4 of *An Historical account of all the Voyages Round the World performed by English navigators including those lately undertaken by Order of his Present Majesty...to which is added an Appendix containing The Journal of a Voyage to the North Pole, by the Hon. Commodore Phipps, and Captain Lutwidge*. (This volume is sometimes referred to as the Newbery narrative after the name of the publisher.) The author, possibly the ship's surgeon William Wallis, referred to himself as a 'journalist'. He was a member of the ship's company of *Carcass* and therefore provides a narrative or 'journal' from the perspective of that vessel. He appears to have accepted the Admiralty's objective, as he suggested that as recent Arctic exploration had left open the question as to 'whether the regions adjoining to the pole are land or water, frozen or open sea', another expedition was necessary to answer this question. It is clear that he saw its value in terms of economic advantage rather than as a scientific quest:

> The advantage of this discovery [of the open polar sea], besides the glory resulting from it...would have been immensely great. To have opened a new channel of commerce at a time when our

trade is languishing would have revived the drooping hopes of our manufacturers, and retained at home the numerous emigrants, who for want of employment in their own country are seeking new habitations, and new means of livings in remote settlements.

He only once made reference to scientific work and that was when the ships were anchored at Fairhaven in north-west Spitsbergen, when he wrote that 'the commanders and officers…busied themselves on making observations… some considerable discussion in the phenomenon of the polar regions may be expected', but he displays no interest in what these might be.

As the Admiralty's objective was doomed to failure, it is for the scientific observations and the scientific appendices in Phipps's narrative that the expedition is best remembered. Phipps, like Joseph Banks before him, created a standard of scientific reporting that subsequent expeditions sought to emulate.

The voyage towards the North Pole

1773 was to be the most memorable year in Skeffington Lutwidge's naval career. By its end he had embarked on a voyage to the North Pole, sailed his ship to the waters north of Spitsbergen, become frozen in, escaped with difficulty from the ice, and had returned to the United Kingdom.

Fitting out at Sheerness

On 21 April 1773 the fitting out of *Carcass* began. The first task was to further strengthen her against the dangers from moving ice. Between 21 and 24 April the hull, keel and stern of the ship were strengthened with oak planks two or more inches thick, new sheathing fixed on to the exterior and additional timbers added in the hold and bows 'to defend her against the ice' (Figures 2.3 and 2.4). As the weeks progressed all the other tasks, necessary for a voyage of up to six months, were carried out. These included painting the vessel (26-27 April), rigging her and bringing on board 25 tons of shingle ballast (3-8 May), stowing water (10 May) and 20 chaldrons of coals 'given by the Government for the Voyage' (11 May), sea victualing (11 May), getting cables on board (12-13 May), stowing the hold (13 May), embarking the guns and gunners' stores (15 May), bending the main sails (15 May), getting the booms on board and bending the small sails (17 May), putting the boatswain's and carpenter's stores on board (18 May), completing placing 34 tons of water on board (19 May), embarking cured beef and pork, peas, oatmeal, rice, tea, sugar, vinegar, mustard, wine and 100 butts of porter 'brewed with the best malt and hops' (21 May), welcoming the French Ambassador on a visit (23 May), getting the launch on board

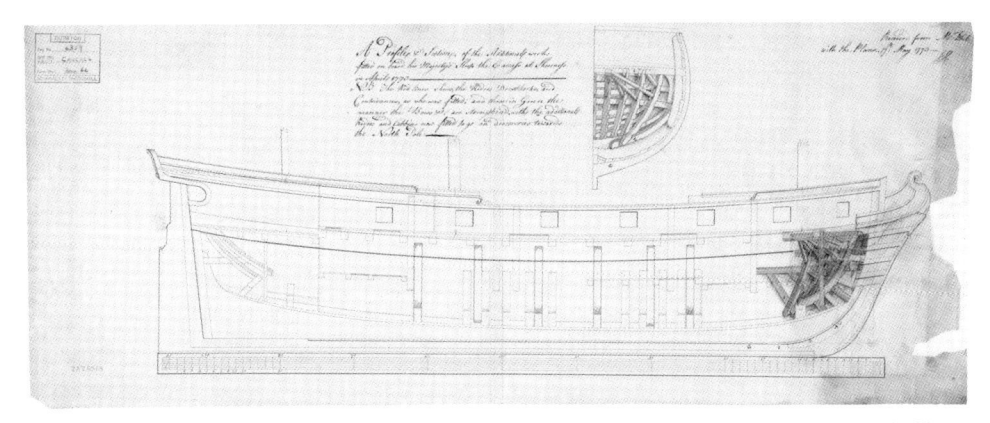

Figure 2.3. 'A profile and section of the additional works fitted on board His Majesty's Sloop the *Carcass* at Sheerness in April 1773'. National Maritime Museum, Admiralty Draughts Collection, No. 6539 *(© National Maritime Museum, Greenwich, London)*

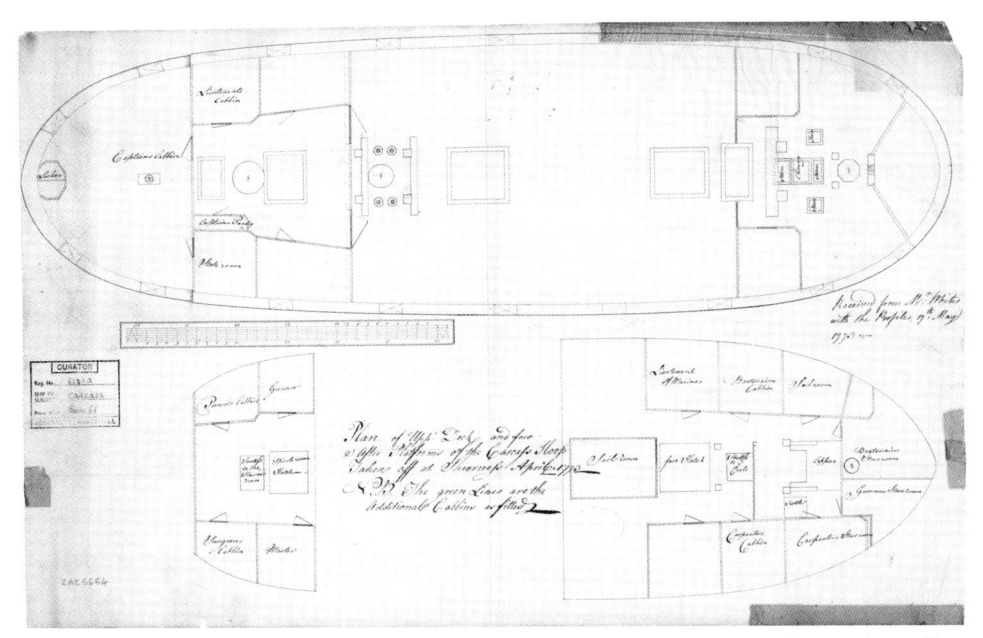

Figure 2.4. 'Plan of Upp. Deck and fore and after platform of the *Carcass* Sloop taken off at Sheerness April 1773'. National Maritime Museum, Admiralty Draughts Collection, No. 4421A *(© National Maritime Museum, Greenwich, London)*

(24 May), and tarring the ship's sides and embarking the clothing provided by the government (25 May). At this point Lutwidge judged the vessel too heavy so he requested that the Admiralty lighten the ship by reducing the complement of men from 90 to 80, and proportionately reducing the stores, as well as by putting six guns on shore, a request that was granted on 27 May. After further work on the "time-keeper" which 'stopt for want of being sufficiently wound up', *Carcass* joined *Racehorse* at the Nore.

The ship's company was primarily drawn from London and the southeast, but with significant contingents from Scotland and Ireland. Apart from Lutwidge himself, only one Cumbrian, an able seaman from Whitehaven called John Robinson, joined the ship for a few weeks while she was being refitted but he did not sail with her. Four whalers with ice-navigation skills were employed as pilots as in March the Navy Board admitted 'that they have not been able to find any Masters in the Navy acquainted in the Greenland Seas'. They thus made provision 'to procure four Persons from the Greenland Ships...[to be employed] in the Capacity as Extra Pilots...at the rate of five shillings a day'. Joshua Edwards and John Preston were to accompany Lutwidge as the pilots in *Carcass*. Floyd commented in his narrative that the 'ice-pilots...having been masters in the Greenland fishing, were not only tolerably well acquainted with the Arctic Seas as far as latitude 82°N, but were dexterous in the steering and general management of shipping amongst the ice'. Lutwidge was aged 36, and the eighty men who eventually sailed north were aged between 16 and 41. Amongst the youngest was the sixteen years old Horatio Nelson, one of a number of young midshipmen on board the vessel (Figure 2.5). Nelson's presence in the ship's company has served both to popularise this voyage and to draw attention away from Lutwidge.

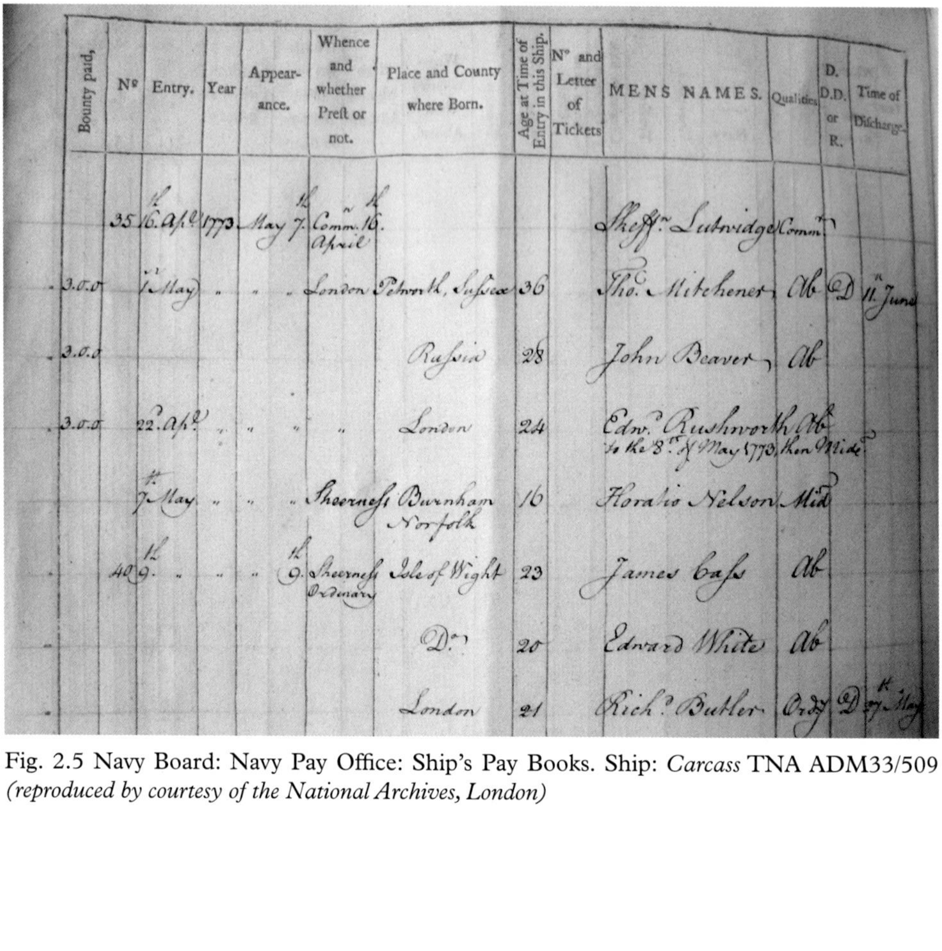

Bounty paid,	No	Entry.	Year	Appearance.	Whence and whether Prest or not.	Place and County where Born.	Age at Time of Entry in this Ship.	No and Letter of Tickets	MENS NAMES.	Qualities	D. D.D. or R.	Time of Discharge
	35	16. Apl	1773	May 7.	Commn 16. April				Sheffn Lutwidge	Comm		
3.0.0		1 May	"	"	London	Petworth, Sussex	36		Thos Mitchener	Ab	D	11 June
3.0.0						Russia	28		John Beaver	Ab		
3.0.0		22 Apl	"	"	"	London	24		Edwd Rushworth to the 8th of May 1773, then Mid	Ab		
		7 May	"	"	Sheerness	Burnham Norfolk	16		Horatio Nelson	Mid		
	40	9.	"	"	9. Sheerness Ordinary	Isle of Wight	23		James Cass	Ab		
						Do	20		Edward White	Ab		
						London	21		Richd Butler	Ordy	D	7 May

Fig. 2.5 Navy Board: Navy Pay Office: Ship's Pay Books. Ship: *Carcass* TNA ADM33/509 *(reproduced by courtesy of the National Archives, London)*

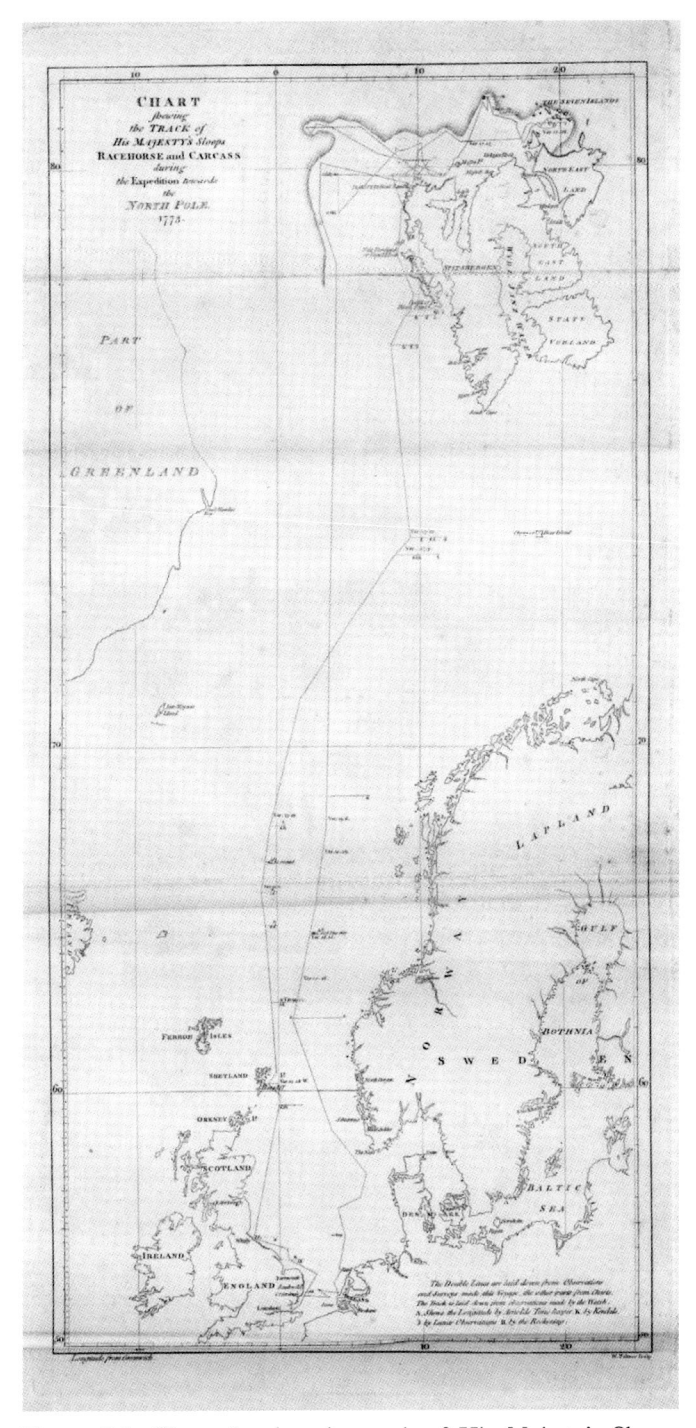

Figure 2.6. Chart showing the track of His Majesty's Sloops *Racehorse* and *Carcass*; Phipps *Voyage*, 1774 *(reproduced by courtesy of Captain Cook Memorial Museum, Whitby)*

THE VOYAGE TO SPITSBERGEN

The two vessels departed from the Nore on 4 June and sailed north along the east coast of Britain calling in at Whitby to take on board further supplies (Figure 2.6). By 16 June they were off the north of Shetland where, because of 'light airs and a thick fog', *Carcass* for a time 'lost sight of the Racehorse who fired guns every half hour'. The following day Lutwidge received his orders from Phipps as to what course of action to take if the ships were separated, a real and worrying possibility in the stormy seas of the North Atlantic. Once out of sight of each other, the chances of effecting a rendezvous would be remote without precise instructions. Consequently Lutwidge's orders were very clear. He was told that 'if the winds should be Easterly to make the best of my way to Trinity (or John Mayen's) Island; if Westerly to Cherry Island' and wait for three days. If Phipps did not arrive within that time 'to make my way to Bell Sound in Spitsbergen', wait for eight days, and if Phipps had not arrived 'to proceed to Hackluit's Headland, waiting in the harbour there until 20th of July; and in case of his not joining me on that day, or within eight days of my arrival there, to open the packet sent with the Mem'l for my further proceedings'. On leaving each of the rendezvous locations, Lutwidge was ordered 'to erect some conspicuous mark and leave a letter informing him [Phipps] of my departure'. In the event these orders remained unused as both vessels sailed in tandem until storms separated them as they returned to England.

On 18 June Lutwidge 'served out to the Ship's Company the Slops [clothing] given by the Government'. This consisted of items considered appropriate for Arctic travel: six fearnaught jackets, two milled caps, two pairs of fearnaught trousers, four pairs of milled stockings, one 'excellent pair of boots', twelve pairs of milled mitts, two cotton shirts and two handkerchiefs for each member of the ship's company. On 20 June both vessels passed the Arctic Circle without ceremony. On 22 June at 70°N 'the weather began to be piercing cold'. By the 25 June they had sailed 805 miles north of Shetland and had reached 74°N and met with 'snow and sleet' for the first time. On 28 June at 77° 30'N, 'a small land bird' was caught on board *Carcass*. The following day, 1060 miles north of Shetland, at '½ past 10pm saw the land of Spitsbergen from ESE to NE about 18 or 20 leagues distance'. The captains 'spoke with the Marquis of Rockingham, Greenlandman…[which] presented each of the commanders with a deer and a half, which they found well-flavoured venison, though not over fat. He informed that he had just come from the ice, and that the day before three whalers had been crushed to pieces by its closing upon them suddenly'. During the following week both vessels sailed north along the west coast of Spitsbergen. Drifting fog was a problem. At '1/2 past 11 came on a thick fog, lost sight of the *Racehorse* which had anchored close inshore. ¾ past 12 heard her Guns which we answered and at 2am got sight of her'. Lutwidge reported seeing large numbers of whaling vessels as they sailed north up the coast. Most of the whaling vessels in that area in 1773 were from Holland, but there were also ships from Hamburg, Bremen and Britain. On 5 July the two ships anchored near Magdalena Hook at nearly 80°N. Lutwidge wrote: 'At 7pm I went on shore from the *Racehorse* with Captn. Phipps who anchored in a small bay and 2 miles from the land. Found it barren, rocky, mountainous and almost covered in snow – a quantity of drift wood on the beach, some of it thrown up much above high water mark. There was a stream of water running down the Mountains from the melted snow, where the *Racehorse's* boat watered' (Figures 2.7 and 2.8).

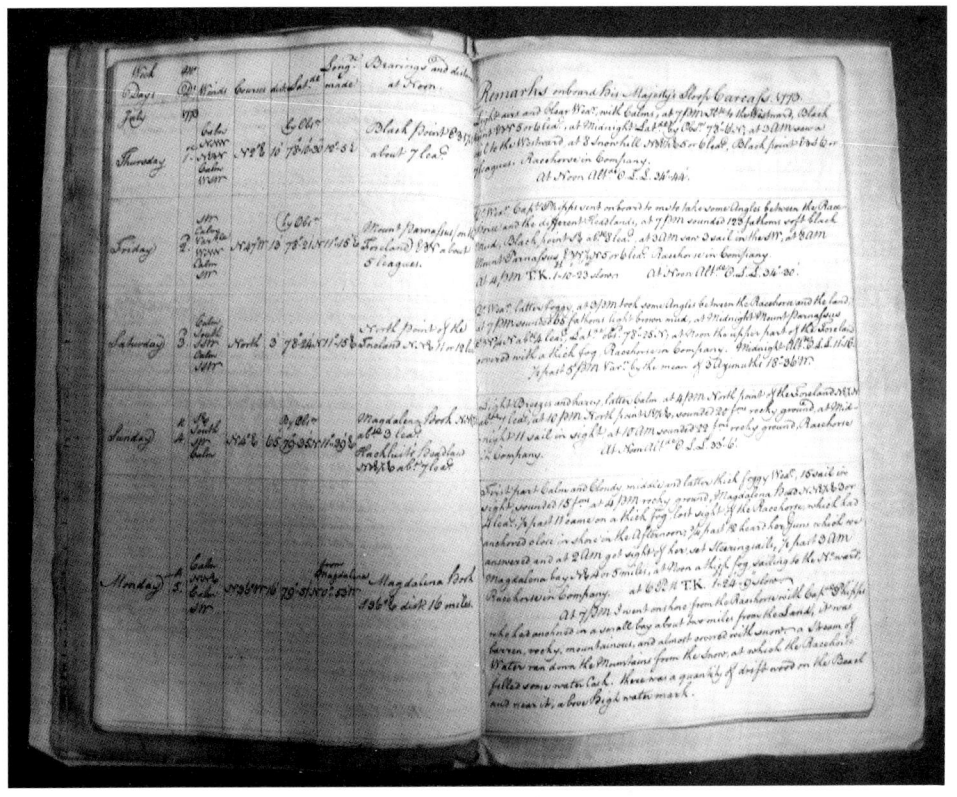

Figure 2.7. A page from Skeffington Lutwidge's journal including the entry for 5 July 1773. TNA ADM55/12 *(reproduced by courtesy of the National Archives, London)*

Figure 2.8. A Spitsbergen beach covered in driftwood (*photograph: Mike Lea*)

NORTH OF SPITSBERGEN

During July both ships operated in the waters to the north of Spitsbergen sailing back and forth along the ice margin searching for leads that could take them further north. The skills of the ice-pilots were especially useful in the areas of drift ice which they encountered. Ice on the move could easily trap and 'nip' a vessel and sink it. On 8 July both ships became beset by ice. 'The ships…were under a necessity of applying to their ice-anchors and poles in order to warp through it'. They used their boats to tow the ships to safety, but *Carcass* suffered some damage when 'she lost her starboard bumpkin and head rails'. On 9 July 'the weather now being piercing cold, the people had an additional quantity of porter and brandy delivered to them'. Unable to proceed north on 9 July both ships retreated to the harbour of Fairhaven at the north-west point of Spitsbergen.

While the vessels were at anchor at Fairhaven time was available to carry out the scientific observations that were of such importance to Phipps and to the Royal Society. The scientific appendices to Phipps's published account include sections on meteorology, natural history, desalination, navigation, refraction and astronomy. Although the reports on meteorology and navigation drew upon the whole voyage, others were largely the result of the time spent at Fairhaven. But as that anonymous 'journalist' on board *Carcass* commented, most of the crew were engaged in readying the ships for the next part of their quest, while the commanders and officers spent their time on science. This suggests that Lutwidge might have taken some part in this work, although Phipps makes no mention that his second-in-command had any scientific role. The 'journalist' explained that while the resupplying and the science were being carried out he 'was employed in surveying the country'. His description of the landscape was typical of how people sought to explain a countryside very different from that with which they were familiar. Lutwidge would probably have described the landscape in similar terms when talking to others about this expedition. The language used was that of the picturesque and the sublime, and comparisons were made to landscape features familiar to a British readership. 'The country has a very awful and romantic appearance...by looking at the hills, a stranger may fancy a thousand different shapes of trees, castles, churches, ruins, ships, whales, monsters and all the various forms that fill the universe'. Like most first-time visitors to the Arctic such as Lutwidge, he also focused on the striking clarity of the atmosphere. The 'journalist' went on to describe the 'astonishing brightness...of the evening rays of the setting sun...a bright blue, like sapphire, and sometimes like the variable colours of a prism, exceeding in lustre the richest gems in the world'. He listed the animals, fish, birds and flora he saw and explains, so far as he understood it, their interesting characteristics and how they lived in the polar environment. He noted the importance of the 'dung of birds', and commented upon the fishiness of the goose and duck eggs that were collected and eaten, and the effect on flowers of the short growing season.

On 19 July the two ships sailed north again, but progress was limited as 'the *Carcass* having several times struck against the ice with such violence, [the latter caused] her head to be raised four feet out of the water'. On the evening of Friday 30 July the ships 'got in amongst the drift ice close to the main body' and two hours later 'there now appeared no open water or passage for the Ships, the main body of the ice seeming to be firmly joined from one island to another'. Because of the lateness of the season there was some degree of alarm and increasing concern as the ice refused to move and their attempts to free themselves failed. The predicament in which they now found themselves caused Lutwidge to write at length in his journal which provides a vivid insight into how the drama developed:

> Saturday 31 July: [Between about midnight and 6.00am] I went in the Boat [the cutter carried on board *Carcass*] to one of these islands [the Seven Islands]...through narrow Channels being obliged to haul the boat over the ice in several places. I had an extensive view of the Sea to the Eastward which was entirely frozen over, not like the ice we had hitherto [encountered],

but a flat even surface as far as the Eye could reach which was undoubtedly 10 leagues at least as the Weather was remarkably fine and clear, and the hill I was upon about 200 yards above the surface of the Sea, a compact body of ice joined to all the Islands and Lands in sight, and no appearance of Water, except the stream along the NE land, the way the Ships came in. There was a great deal of driftwood upon this Island, some of it thrown up much higher than high water mark, and some Cask Staves which had also been thrown up by the Sea, many Dears Horns lying upon the ground, and the marks of Bears and Dears feet everywhere amongst the snow. This island is three or four miles long, very hilly, and no appearance of any Verdure except in some small spots amongst the broken precipices.

Sunday 1 August: Laying fast amongst the drift ice, and at 4pm made fast the Ship to it, and filled all our water Casks from a pool upon the ice. 10pm cast the Ship loose and made fast to the ice near the *Racehorse*. At 11am a large white Bear coming over the ice towards the Ships, was shot and brought on board the *Racehorse*. These bears are very good eating, and where no better is to be purchased, the whalers account them as good as beef.

Monday 2 August: Both ships clearly beset with the ice and no possibility of moving them, as the Wind blew directly in from the open water which was now 7 or 8 miles distant to the Westward.

Tuesday 3 August: am both Ships Companies employed with the Ice Saws and Axes in endeavouring to cut a passage thro' the ice for the Ships to haul thro' to the Westward, the *Carcass* made fast to the stern of the *Racehorse*. The Weather was remarkably warm at noon, the Tar running upon the Side.

Wednesday 4 August: pm the people employed from both Ships as in the morning cutting thro' the ice ahead of the *Racehorse*, found it answered no purpose as we did not advance above two or three Ships lengths thro' the ice during the whole day, and the Ships were still drifting to the Eastward; some of the ice we cut thro' was eight feet thick.

Thursday 5 August: The Ships still drifting to the Eastward; am kill'd three bears upon the ice from the Ship.

Friday 6 August: Foggy. At 2pm sent one of the Pilots to the West Island to view the ice, and see how far distant the open water was from the Ships. At 7pm observed the ice open a little but it soon closed again.

Saturday 7 August: Latter part thick foggy weather with snow and sleet. The Pilot who went to the West Island found the nearest open water was...above five leagues distant from the Ships. pm hoisted out all the Boats upon the ice, the people employed in fitting them, making and filling small bags small Bread bags, dressing provisions etc. Capt. Phipps being resolved to endeavour to save the people by pushing over to Hakluyt's Headland, and getting on board the Dutch Ships before they left that part of Spitsbergen, unless the ice opened very soon. am employed as before; found the Ships still kept drifting to the Eastward with the body of ice that enclosed them, one piece pressing upon another and rising in heaps all round them, occasioned undoubtedly by the Westerly Winds driving it on to the Eastward where it was stopp'd by the Islands and the fix'd frozen Sea behind. At noon got the Launches completed and moved them along a little way to the Westward to try how they would haul over the ice, intending to quit the Ships as soon as we had got them along a few miles towards the open water, if the ice did not open in the meantime [Figure 2.9]. There appeared no probability of the Ships getting out this Year as the Season was so far advanced, and if we attempted wintering, it would be impossible to prevent their being crushed by the ice as they were at so great a distance from the Land.

Sunday 8 August: ½ past Noon finding the ice slack a little, the Racehorse set her Sails endeavouring to press thro' it, the Carcass still fast astern of her. At 3pm the people returned from getting the Launches along to the Westward. At 6pm both Ships stop'd again by the ice, having got a little way thro' it. At 4am found the ice press hard upon the ship; at 11 sent the 2nd and 3rd Lieutenants with 50 men to haul the Launch over the ice to the Westward. At Noon found the ice opening a little and the Ships moving with it about a mile an hour to the Westward.

At this point the anonymous 'journalist' on *Carcass* took the opportunity to praise the leadership of Skeffington Lutwidge. 'When [the hauliers] returned to the ships, Captain Lutwidge, who was no less loved by his men than the Commodore, had by his example and his judicious direction done wonders. Both ships were not only afloat, with their sails set, but actually cut and warped through the ice near half a mile'.

Figure 2.9. View of the *Racehorse* and *Carcass,* 7 August 1773: based on the engraving by John Cleveley, Hauling boats over the ice off Spitsbergen, August 7th, 1773 *(© National Maritime Museum, Greenwich, London)*

In continuing the journal Lutwidge describes how changing weather and ice conditions enabled the vessels to escape from the pack ice:

> Monday 9 August: pm forcing the Ships through the ice; at 6pm the party returned from the Launches which they had haul'd over the ice 3 or 4 miles to the Westward. At 8pm cast loose from the Racehorse and set the Sails to follow her. At 4am saw the Launches ahead through the fog; employ'd in warping through the ice which was very close and heavy, but we found the Ships move along with it to the Westward.

> Tuesday 10 August: First part Calm with light airs and fog; middle part light airs with much Snow. Latter Fresh Breezes and hazy with Snow. At 9pm sent 25 men with an officer to bring the Launch on board as we found the Ships getting fast on to the Westward. At 1am got the Launch alongside. At Noon the ice opening very much and the Ships getting fast along to the Westward

Wednesday 11 August: Sailing amongst loose ice to the Westward. ½ past 1pm set Steering Sails, being in open water. At 10 hoisted in the Launch which had been hung in the Tackles, and lashed alongside.

The predicament in which the ships found themselves during the first week of August was not only apparent to the commanders and officers. On *Racehorse* the ex-slave Olaudah Equiano, perhaps the first African to visit the Arctic, wrote that 'our situation [was] very dreadful and alarming…we were in very great apprehension of having the ships squeezed to pieces'.

Lutwidge's journal did not even mention the event on 4 August that has become the best-known moment on the entire journey. He may have been too preoccupied with the increasingly precarious situation, but on that day, according to the numerous biographers of Nelson including Robert Southey, writing in Keswick in 1813, Midshipman Horatio Nelson and the coxswain of *Carcass* ventured onto the ice, armed only with a musket, and encountered a polar bear which fortunately was separated from them by 'a chasm in the ice'. The predicament of the two was spotted from the *Carcass* and guns were fired to scare off the bear (Figure 2.10). Nelson later explained himself to Lutwidge by saying: 'Sir, I wished to kill the bear, that I may carry its skin to my father'. Nelson never mentioned this story, and it is possible that there is no truth in it, but as will be shown in Chapter 7, this event, and the ways it was illustrated, influenced the way Cumbrians and others imagined the Arctic.

Figure 2.10. 'Nelson and the Bear' by Richard Westall, c1806 *(©National Maritime Museum, Greenwich, London)*

The return to England

Once free of the ice both ships returned to Fairhaven for the ships' companies to recover, before Phipps ordered the vessels to return to England. As they sailed south towards Shetland and the Scottish coast the ships ran into violent autumn gales. Phipps described the period from 7 to 24 September as one of 'hard gales with little intermission…in one of these gales, the hardest, I think, I was ever in, and with the greatest sea, we lost three of our boats [and] had been obliged to heave all their guns overboard, except two'. On 11 September the vessels separated in a storm and did not meet up again until they reached Harwich. The 'journalist' wrote that at this time *Carcass* 'shipped such heavy seas, it washed all the provisions and casks that were lashed on the deck, overboard; they kept two pumps going; and were obliged to scuttle the boats, to prevent them being washed overboard.' At four in the morning of the 12th he reported that the sea 'washed all booms and spars that had been with all possible care secured on the deck, overboard. The ship mostly under water'. On 13 September *Carcass* put in at Yarmouth Roads, and as Lutwidge did not know of the fate of *Racehorse*, he 'sent away an Express to the Admiralty with a Journal of the Proceedings of the Voyage'. His accompanying letter made it clear that as 'Captn. Phipps has done everything possible (tho' without effect) to accomplish a passage Northwards', [it can reasonably be concluded that] 'it is impossible to proceed further than we did towards the North Pole on the West side of Spitsbergen'.

The other 'journalists' on board concurred. The anonymous Newbery author wrote that 'there does not appear the least reason to conclude that any practicable passage to the Indian Ocean can ever be found in this direction, for were it certain that the seas were always open under the pole, yet great bulwarks of ice evidently surround it'. Equiano, very much out of his element in the Arctic, agreed: 'we fully proved the impracticability of finding a passage that way to India'. Some of the newspapers that reported on the return of the expedition confirmed that there would be no second attempt. For example, the *Caledonian Mercury* wrote: 'We are informed that Government will not fit out any more vessels on these northern expeditions'.

Despite this expedition's experience, a belief in the open polar sea persisted. Sir John Barrow, the champion of Arctic exploration during the first half of the nineteenth century, believed in it and a 'distinguished German geographer' was still advocating its existence in 1876. Although the expedition inevitably could not achieve its geographical objective, its significance lay in its scientific work. The scientific appendices to Phipps's narrative of the voyage set the standard for scientific reporting for years to come. The discovery of the Ivory Gull *(Pagophila eburnea)*, and the first adequate description of the polar bear were amongst the achievements of this expedition. In addition the expedition reached a new furthest north on

27 July 1773 of 80° 48'N. This was not surpassed until William Scoresby Sr. reached 81° 30'N in 1816.

SKEFFINGTON LUTWIDGE, HOLMROOK HALL AND HIS FINAL YEARS IN CUMBERLAND

Lutwidge never returned to the Arctic. In some ways this is surprising because of the Admiralty's commitment to further Arctic exploration in the North West Passage from 1776 and the small number of officers with ice-navigation experience. In 1776 James Cook and Charles Clerke embarked on a voyage to try to establish a North West Passage from west to east, from the Bering Strait to Baffin Bay, and in the same year the Admiralty sent Richard Pickersgill (and, the following year, Walter Young) to Davis Strait and Baffin Bay to conduct surveys in advance of Cook's possible arrival from the west. Cook had experience of ice in Antarctica and elsewhere, but given the regions in which these expeditions were operating, Lutwidge's expertise might have been useful. However, with the outbreak of the American War of Independence in 1775, Lutwidge had been sent to North America, and was not available to join the expeditions of 1776.

Lutwidge continued his career in the Royal Navy, joining the Mediterranean Fleet with the outbreak of the French Revolutionary War in 1793, and subsequently serving in home waters and being promoted to admiral of the blue in 1801 with HMS *Overyssel* as his flagship. He appears to have retired from active service in January 1802, and was further promoted to admiral of the white in 1805 and admiral of the red in 1810.

In around 1800 Lutwidge came to live at the Holmrook Hall estate, near Gosforth, which had been bought by his eldest brother Charles (1722-1784) in 1759. Charles had used it as a summer residence and had enlarged both the house and the estate. He had acquired fishing rights on the River Calder and was Lord of the Manor of Bolton, Gosforth and Newton with Seascales, and he had the Right of Presentations to the Parish Church in Gosforth. At various times he was a Deputy Lieutenant for Cumberland, a magistrate, 'Surveyor and Comptroller of the Coasts of Cumberland and Westmorland', and 'Surveyor General of Customs in Cumberland, Westmorland and Lancaster'. He was clearly a man of some significance locally. He died without issue, and the estate was inherited by his younger brother Henry (1724-1798). In 1794, William Hutchinson in *The History of the County of Cumberland* described the property as 'standing on the north banks of the river Irt; much modern improvement is seen about it, good gardens and pleasant walks'. Henry's eldest son, Major Charles Lutwidge (1768-1848), inherited the estate, the fishery and the lordships of the manors on his father's death in 1798, but living in London he had no interest in Cumberland, and within a couple of years Holmrook was sold to Charles's great uncle, Admiral Skeffington Lutwidge. Lutwidge was also associated with other properties as according to the 1800 edition of Peter Crosthwaite's map of Windermere his name was linked to a property named Greenbank near Storrs Hall, and at the same time he owned a London house at 17 Argyll Street, the contents of which he insured through Sun Insurance. Given his age and his affection for Holmrook, that house became his home, but he seems to have retained his interest in Greenbank until at least 1809, as well as Argyll Street which he continued to insure until 1812.

There is no record of the extent of the Holmrook estate, or the layout of the hall, at this time. However by 1923, when Col. E.F. Lowthorpe-Lutwidge sold the estate, it consisted of the hall, gardens and woods extending to 54 acres, while the whole estate amounted to 369 acres. This included two farms – Cookson Place Farm and Kirkland Farm. The house had been built in the eighteenth century with later additions and alterations. The principal rooms included the Lounge Hall with Adam wood mantel and overmantel; the Terrace Hall with a door onto the Terrace Verandah, with walls relieved by Adam decoration; the Elliptical Dining Room with walls with a wood dado surmounted by plaster panels with Adam decorations and cornices, and a marble mantel with Adam decoration; a library, gun room, drying room, a school room, a handsome carved staircase, an elliptical drawing room (with ornamental inlaid white and coloured marble mantel with Adam scroll

Figure 2.11. The front elevation of Holmrook Hall in the early 1940s. The photograph was taken by the late Lt. Peter Friend (RNVR), Chief Instructor at HMS *Volcano*. The photograph is courtesy of his son, Michael Friend of South Carolina. Photograph via Sheila Ann Cartwright Cumbria Image Bank. *(reproduced by courtesy of Cumbria County Council, Carlisle Library)*

Figure 2.12. The surviving gate to the stable yard *(photograph: Rob David)*

decorations, black and steel fireplace with original porcelain panels, dado, cornice, enriched domed ceiling, curved mahogany door with ornamental curved head), boudoir, billiard room, nine principal bedrooms, 2 dressing rooms, 7 secondary and servants' bedrooms, a housemaid's room, and the usual domestic offices. Outside there was stabling and a stable yard, farm buildings and grounds which included a shrubbery, ornamental woodlands and a walled vegetable garden (Figures 2.11, 2.12 and 2.13).

It is unclear how much time Lutwidge spent at Holmrook but in 1806 his young wife, Catherine, the daughter of Richard Bateson of Londonderry, was in residence when she received a letter from Emma Hamilton, in mourning after Nelson's death. It was written on 10 February 1806 and addressed to 'Mrs Admiral Lutwidge': 'What can I say to my dearest friend….Nelson is dead and has left me most forlorn, but his last breath was for me….all is a void, all seems dark and comfortless to me. When do you come to Town, that will be some comfort to me, that we may speak, think, weep and grieve

Figure 2.13. The gardener's cottage and the walled garden *(photograph: Rob David)*

together for the loss of this dear ever to be lamented friend. May God bless you and your excellent Admiral. Write to your poor afflicted heart-broken Emma'.

When Lutwidge died in August 1814 aged 78, the obituary in the *Cumberland Pacquet* (23 August 1814) commented that he was beloved and respected by those under his command, but even on this occasion he remained in the shadow of his midshipman, Nelson, as the only reference that was made to his career was that he 'was the first Naval Preceptor of Lord Nelson'. He died without issue, leaving three guineas per annum, charged upon land, to be distributed annually at Christmas amongst six poor widows of the parish of Irton. The Holmrook estate was bequeathed to his nephew Major Skeffington Lutwidge DL (1779-1854) who served with distinction in India. Like many manor houses where the direct succession failed, the property was abandoned by the family and the furniture removed or sold, and the house rented out. A few items survived including a gold snuff box which had belonged to Lutwidge and was inherited by Charles Robert Fletcher Lutwidge in 1861. Holmrook Hall was demolished in 1956.

Figure 2.14. Irton Church *(photograph: Rob David)*

Admiral Skeffington Lutwidge was buried at Irton Church (Figure 2.14). The memorial in the north aisle (Figure 2.15), makes particular reference to the 'Voyage of Discovery towards the North Pole' and ignores the other naval commands he held, clearly indicating that it was the voyage of 1773 that was seen as defining his career.

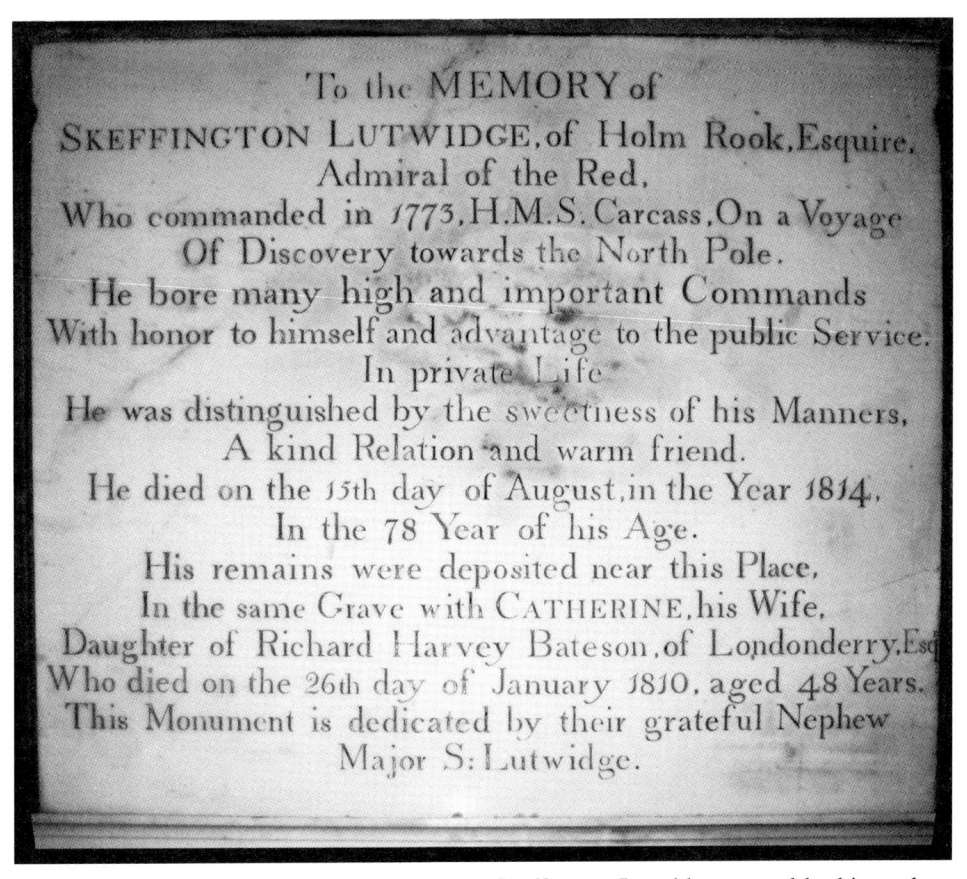

Figure 2.15. Part of the memorial to Admiral Skeffington Lutwidge erected by his nephew Major Skeffington Lutwidge at Irton Church *(photograph: Rob David)*

★ ★ ★ ★ ★

SUGGESTED FURTHER READING

Anonymous, *An Historical account of all the Voyages Round the World performed by English navigators including those lately undertaken by Order of his Present Majesty… to which is added an Appendix containing The Journal of a Voyage to the North Pole, by the Hon. Commodore Phipps, and Captain Lutwidge,Vol.4,* (London, F. Newbery, 1774).

J. Barrow, *A Chronological History of the Voyages into the Arctic Regions*, (London, John Murray, 1818. Reprinted: Newton Abbot, David and Charles, 1971).

E. C. Coleman, *The Royal Navy in Polar Exploration from Frobisher to Ross*, (Stroud, Tempus, 2006).

A. H. Markham, *Northward Ho: including a Narrative of Captain Phipps's Expedition by a Midshipman [Thomas Floyd]*, (London, Macmillan, 1879).

Northward Ho! A Voyage Towards the North Pole, (Catalogue to the exhibition at the Captain Cook Memorial Museum, Whitby, 2010).

C. J. Phipps, *A Voyage Towards the North Pole undertaken by His Majesty's command 1773*, (London, J. Nourse, 1774).

A. Savours, '"A Very Interesting Point in Geography": the 1773 Phipps Expedition to the North Pole', *Arctic*, 37:4 (Dec. 1984), 402-428.

G. Williams, *The Search for the North West Passage in the Age of Reason*, (London, HarperCollins, 2002).

Chapter 3
'For sale: a quantity of whale oil':
Whaling from Whitehaven 1762-1791

Whitehaven and Whitehaven-built ships were involved in the Northern Whale Fishery, as Arctic whaling was known, for just over one hundred years, from 1762 to 1863. Before then Cumbrians occasionally made use of whale meat and whale oil from stranded whales. For example, on four occasions in May 1307, whale meat, presumably salted or smoked, was provided for Edward I's court at Carlisle. The accounts do not state where the whale meat came from, but it may well have been from a whale stranded on the sands of the Solway Firth. We know from a letter sent by William Gilpin, Sir John Lowther's steward, that in 1694 two whales which had beached at Flimby were illegally seized by local freeholders who 'made about £20 [from] the oil'. Nearly seventy years later Whitehaven became directly involved in the Northern Whale Fishery. In the 1760s, 1780s and 1790s a small number of vessels left Whitehaven for the Greenland Sea to the east of Greenland to return with whale oil and whale bone. The port continued its involvement into the nineteenth century through building vessels that became whalers at other ports.

Whitehaven's merchants were persuaded to send *Royal Bounty* to the Arctic for a number of years in the early 1760s as a consequence of the loss of the tobacco trade to Glasgow during the 1750s, and because of a government bounty designed to encourage expansion in the whaling trade, payable to whale ships according to their tonnage. Later in the century, competition for the coal trade from other Cumbrian ports and the continuation of the bounty led to a number of Whitehaven ships being fitted out for whaling during the 1780s and 1790s. Two of these vessels, *Thompson* and *Precedent*, were Whitehaven built. However, the national expansion of the whaling industry during the 1780s led to a glut of whale oil and to lower prices, and these were major factors in the eventual demise of the industry at smaller whaling ports such as Whitehaven during the 1790s. However, it was not until 1863 that the last Whitehaven-built whaling ship, *Jumna*, was crushed by ice in Melville Bay (see Chapter 4).

The 1760s

By the end of the 1740s, declining catches of the Bowhead or Greenland Right whale (*Balaena mysticetus*) in the Greenland Sea caused the Dutch, who had dominated the European whaling trade, to withdraw. The Greenland Right was 'right for all the wrong reasons'. It was a docile, slow-moving giant, up to sixty feet long with a thick layer of blubber and large quantities of baleen in the mouth. Its greatest advantage over many other whale species was that it floated when killed, and thus was relatively easy to tow towards the mother ship for flensing. During the 1740s the British government, concerned by the country's dependence upon imported whale products, increased the bounty payable to whale ships. This bounty was seen as a way of making Britain less dependent upon imported oil and of expanding the fleet and thus the country's defence capability, as whaling was considered to be an excellent training ground for British sailors. Consequently in 1749 the government raised the bounty on whale ships from 30s. per ship ton to 40s. per ship ton. As whaling was such an uncertain occupation, this enhanced bounty gave shipowners the financial incentive to invest in, and equip, whaling ships. Little infrastructure was needed to refine whale oil and to process whale bone, since simple, temporary facilities to render the blubber were adequate. Consequently many ports, including Whitehaven, seized the opportunity to become involved in whaling.

In 1762 a 229 tons London-listed ship, *Royal Bounty*, was fitted out at Whitehaven to be 'employed in the Whale Fishery to Davis's Streights and the Greenland Seas' (Figure 3.4). As there was a dispute over the ship's tonnage, on which the bounty would be based, she was only granted a licence on 29 July which resulted in her late departure to the fishing grounds. Unfortunately 1762 was a poor whaling year with the British fleet taking only 22 whales, so it was not surprising that the *Royal Bounty* caught only 11 seals which produced merely a quarter of a ton of blubber. Although 1763 was a more successful year for the British fleet with 115 whales and 707 seals caught, producing in total 1495 tons of blubber, *Royal Bounty* once again enjoyed only limited success. She caught one and a half whales (which meant that the catch of one of the whales had involved another ship, and the carcass was shared between them) which produced sixteen and a half tons of blubber. *Royal Bounty* appears to have sailed again in 1764, but after that date there is no further record of any ship sailing from Whitehaven to the Northern Whale Fishery until 1785. The blubber and whale bone brought back by *Royal Bounty* were probably processed elsewhere, so that Whitehaven's first involvement with the whaling industry would have left little mark on the town.

THE 1770S AND EARLY 1780S

Presumably some of the ship's company of *Royal Bounty* had been recruited in Whitehaven. We know that during the 1770s and early 1780s there were further opportunities for Whitehaven mariners to participate in the whaling trade, not at Whitehaven, but at Liverpool. The Liverpool whaling ships, *Golden Lion* (310 tons) and *Lion* (300 tons), both part of Thomas Staniforth's fleet, acquired a significant proportion of their crews from Whitehaven between 1772 and 1784 (Figure 3.1). In 1776, for example, twenty-five of the ship's company of fifty-two in *Golden Lion* were signed on at Whitehaven on 28 February and sailed to Liverpool where the rest of the crew were engaged on 3 March. *Golden Lion* was then at sea until 14 August, an unusually long whaling season of over five months. On 22 August the *Cumberland Pacquet* reported: 'Arrived at Liverpool, the *Golden Lion*, [Richard] Thompson [master], from Greenland with 1 fish and 800 seals – the seamen who belong to this port arrived here Tuesday [20 August]'. Between 1772 and 1780 the number of Whitehaven crew members on the *Golden Lion* never fell below eleven, and although many seamen only signed on for single voyages, several gained experience over a number of seasons. Joseph Coulthard, Robert Fleming, John Hewer and Henry Jackson, for example, sailed to the Arctic in every year between 1776 and 1780. From 1781 *Golden Lion* sailed to the West Indies, but Thompson continued to sail to the Arctic between 1782 and 1784 as master of *Lion*, although the number of Whitehaven mariners who were hired did not rise above six. Robert Fleming and a number of other mariners followed Thompson from *Golden Lion* to *Lion*. Between 1774 and 1784 over ninety Whitehaven sailors gained experience of the Arctic and whaling, and they no doubt became the nucleus of the ships' companies when whaling began again in Whitehaven in 1785. It can have been no coincidence that the last year that Whitehaven sailors signed on as crew in Liverpool whaling vessels was in the previous year, 1784. Unfortunately it is not possible to know the roles played by the Whitehaven mariners on board those Liverpool ships, but with up to half the crew coming from the town, it is likely that some of the specialists on board were Whitehaven men. In 1778 and 1779, Robert Sheridan was a member of the ship's company of *Golden Lion*, and he may be the same Captain Sheridan who later became master of *Lonsdale*, Whitehaven's first whaling vessel, in 1785.

Although Whitehaven was the hub of Cumbria's whaling industry, in 1781 two Workington sailors joined the Liverpool whaling ship *Betty*, and during the mid-1770s John Spedding of Armathwaite and Mirehouse invested in whaling and appears to have been part-owner of the whaling ship *Neptune*. This was probably the Liverpool-registered *Neptune* that successfully sailed to the Northern Whale Fishery in 1776 and 1777, but was wrecked in the

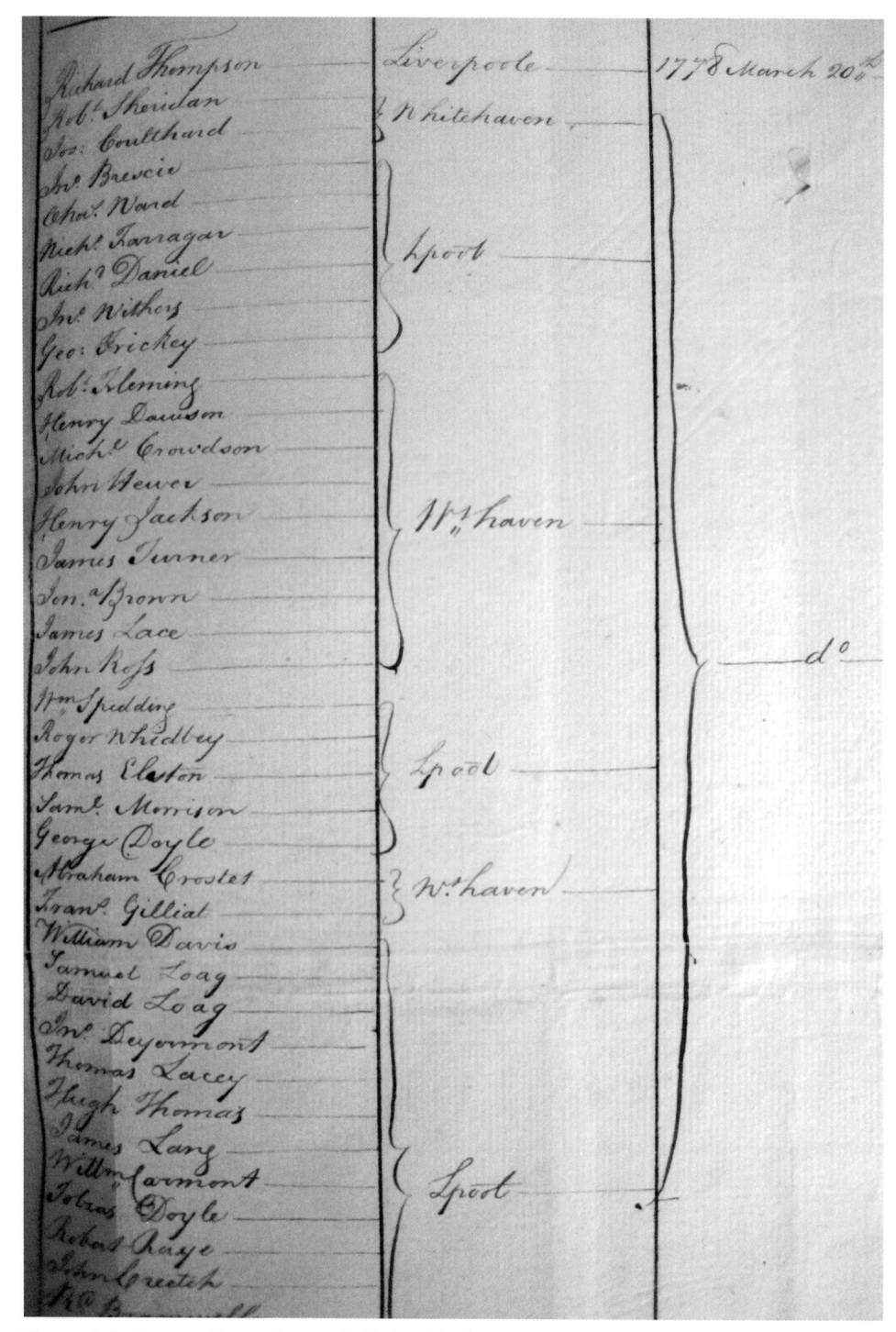

Figure 3.1. Extract from Muster Roll for *Golden Lion* sailing from Liverpool, 1778. TNA BT98/38 *(reproduced by courtesy of the National Archives, London)*

Figure 3.2. *Neptune* whaling in the East Greenland Sea 1778 *(reproduced by courtesy of Mr J. Spedding, Mirehouse: photograph: Julian Sale)*

Arctic in 1778. The two paintings of this vessel at Mirehouse provide a vivid record of whaling and its dangers (Figures 3.2 and 3.3). One of the paintings depicts a successful whale catch in which the men in the whale boats cheer their success, and the crew on board *Neptune* are shown flensing a whale. The second painting depicts the ship's destruction, squeezed between two ice floes. The ship's company is shown on the ice along with the equipment they

Figure 3.3. *Neptune* nipped by ice in the East Greenland Sea 1778 *(reproduced by courtesy of Mr J. Spedding, Mirehouse: photograph: Julian Sale)*

have been able to offload. They have saved the blubber which was stored in the barrels as well as the whaleboats which will become their means of escape if they are not rescued from the ice by another whaleship. Fortunately for the shipwrecked ship's company another vessel was nearby, so they were rescued. This ship is depicted in the background of Figure 3.3. Although *Neptune* sailed from Liverpool with a crew composed entirely of Liverpool men, John Spedding may have been encouraged in his part-ownership of this whaling vessel by Whitehaven's earlier involvement in the trade. The loss of the ship would have highlighted the risks involved in investing in whaling, so would have done little to encourage other Whitehaven or Cumbrian investors at that time.

THE LATE 1780S AND 1790S

During the 1770s the bounty had been reduced to 30*s*. per ton but in 1782 it was once again increased to 40*s*. per ton. This increase, alongside the reduced participation of the Dutch fleet and the end of the American war in 1783, acted as a catalyst for the revival of the whaling industry nationally. By 1788 there were 253 whaling ships being fitted out at British ports, the largest number of vessels Britain ever sent to the Arctic. Whitehaven was part of this expansion, and the first of the new Whitehaven ships, *Lonsdale*, made her maiden voyage to the whale fishery in 1785 (Figure 3.4).

Unusually, *Lonsdale* was solely owned by an aristocrat, Sir James Lowther, Earl of Lonsdale, after whom she was named. Few aristocrats invested in whaling, and given the cost of refitting a ship for the whaling trade and the inherent dangers, it was rare for whaling vessels to be owned by a single person, but Sir James was not short of money. It is likely that he was encouraged by the opportunity to sell whale oil to the Whitehaven harbour commissioners for their new street lighting. Although there had been an intention to light the streets in 1761, nothing happened until 1781 when the town's streets were lit with oil lamps, presumably with whale oil brought from elsewhere. The *Cumberland Pacquet* reported in 1786 the intention to construct a whale-processing facility in the town – 'a place for boiling the blubber, it is said, will be immediately prepared'. It is likely that this facility would have been similar to the temporary structure which was built on Parton beach in 1787. We know that it was constructed, as the newspaper was soon reporting that 'some of the blubber brought by the *Lonsdale* is now boiling for the lamps of the town'.

Lonsdale, at 263 tons, was amongst the smaller ships fitted out for the Northern Whale Fishery. She was a three-masted, square-sterned ship which had been built at Norfolk, Virginia in 1774. She sailed from Whitehaven in both 1785 and 1786. In 1785, she departed for Greenland on 23 March under the command of Captain Sheridan. She left the ice for her return voyage to Whitehaven on 10 August and arrived at the port on 22 August with about 200 seals but no whales. It had not been a good season for *Lonsdale* or the British fleet, but despite this the Earl of Lonsdale quickly indicated his intention to send *Lonsdale* to the Arctic in 1786. She sailed in early April under the command of Captain John Gordon and returned to considerable acclaim in mid-August. The *Cumberland Pacquet* reported:

> The *Lonsdale*, Gordon, from Greenland. Her arrival with the first whales ever brought into the port of Whitehaven, was celebrated by firing two field pieces from the North Wall, for which purpose the gentlemen volunteers of the artillery company had mustered, and made the necessary preparations. The *Lonsdale* left the ice on the 12th of July, and has brought the produce of two fish and forty seals.

Lonsdale was re-registered at Whitehaven in 1787, and John Gordon was once again named as master. However, there is no evidence that she sailed to Greenland in that year, perhaps because the declining value of whale oil alongside the reduction in the bounty to 30s. per ton made the trade less attractive to her owner. In 1788 she was broken up at Whitehaven.

Lonsdale's success in 1786 had, however, prompted a small increase in the size of the Whitehaven whaling fleet in 1787. *Thompson* (221 tons, 2 decks, 3 masts, 85ft long and 25ft broad) had been built and fitted out in late 1777 or early 1778 by the Whitehaven shipbuilders William Bowes and Sons, and *Pollux* (renamed *Precedent* – 301 tons) had been built for the Whitehaven merchant Daniel Brocklebank by the local shipbuilding firm of Spedding and Co. in 1780. These were the first Whitehaven-built ships to become whalers (Figure 3.4).

Shortly after her construction, *Thompson* had been set ablaze by the American privateer John Paul Jones who landed at Whitehaven on 23 April 1778. The damage to the vessel was not too extensive as 'immediately after the alarm was given, the fire engines were brought to the quay, and by the vigorous exertions of people of all ranks, the fire was speedily extinguished, without damaging any other vessel', and she was quickly rebuilt. Sailing from Bristol she became involved in trade with the American colonies, but in April 1785 she returned to Whitehaven and was fitted out for the Northern Whale Fishery. In 1787 she was registered at Whitehaven, and like most ships of that time she was in multiple ownership. She had three subscribing and nine non-subscribing owners including a number of merchants and people associated with shipping at the port, as well as Joseph Bell, her master on her last voyage to Virginia and on her Greenland voyages.

Ships built at Whitehaven for the Americas trade would not have survived an encounter with the Arctic pack ice without considerable modification. Accessing the government bounty required whaling vessels to be 'strongly built and a proper ship for such voyage and fishery'. William Scoresby, the most famous whaling master of the era, believed that Greenland ships 'should admeasure 3-400 tons; built of the best and strongest material. Flush-decked; hold beams laying low the better to resist a pressure of ice. A flat-floored burdensome hold, for good stowage and carrying a large cargo...'. The process of refitting would have been unfamiliar to the Whitehaven shipwrights, so the work may have been undertaken elsewhere. The most important work involved strengthening their hulls to withstand the relentless pressure of the pack ice. This required covering the hull with a second layer of oak planks, two inches thick, with a third layer at the bow. In addition the bow and stern would have been fortified with thick oak beams and sheathed on the outside with iron plates. This would not have made either ship beautiful to look at, but it would have meant that they were fit for purpose – 'broad of beam to carry a sixty ton animal alongside, thick-skinned to absorb collision with the rock-hard ice, rigged for ease of handling in the unpredictable northern waters when all but a handful of men were away in pursuit of a whale'. They would also have to be redesigned internally to provide the 'flat-floored burdensome hold' to stow the whale bone and the barrels containing the blubber as well as to provide space for a ship's company of about fifty (compared to less than half that figure when they were employed in the Americas trade), and provisions for a voyage of up to eight months. In addition space had to be found on her decks for six open boats used for the actual whale hunt. The cost of fitting out was substantial. A figure of £12-12-0 per ton for a second-hand vessel was considered reasonable in 1786, which would have meant that *Thompson* would have cost £2784 and *Precedent* £3792. It was not surprising therefore that most whale ships were in multiple ownership.

Thompson and *Precedent* required licences to fish in 'the Whale Fishery of the Greenland Seas'. Those for 1789 and 1790 record the granting of individual certificates for the six whaleboats (boats up to about 27 feet long with crews of six) which were used to hunt a whale once it had been sighted. Neither muster rolls nor crew lists have survived, but it can be surmised that as well as the master, a mate and a surgeon, the ship's company of about fifty would have included specialists such as the spectioneer, harpooners, boatsteerers and line managers. In addition there would have been a cook, carpenters and coopers and about twenty seamen and two or three apprentices. Who these people were is unknown, although some may have served previously in *Golden Lion* and *Lion*. The parish registers are silent and the only reference is a newspaper announcement of the marriage of 'Mr Brown, Harpooner of the ship *Precedent* of this port to Miss Wilson of Ginns' in August 1789.

Date	Vessel	Tonnage	Master	Catch and other information
1762	*Royal Bounty*	229 tons		Seals – 11
1763	*Royal Bounty*			Whales – 1.5
1764	*Royal Bounty*			There is no information about this voyage
1785	*Lonsdale*	263 tons	Captain Sheridan	Seals – 200
1786	*Lonsdale*		John Gordon	Whales – 2 Seals – 40
1787	*Precedent* (Built at Whitehaven 1780)	301 tons	Joseph Benn	Whales – 6 Seals – 3 (20 according to *Cumberland Pacquet*) Blubber – 21.5 tons Bear skin - 1
	Thompson (Built at Whitehaven 1777/78)	221 tons	Joseph Bell	Whales – 1 Blubber – 16.5 tons
1788	*Precedent*			Whales – 2 Seals – 17 Unicorns (narwhal) – 1 Seahorses (walrus) – 4
	Thompson			Whales – 4 Seals - 28 Unicorns (narwhal) – 4 Bears – 2
1789	*Precedent*		Joseph Benn	Whales – 10 Seals - 832
	Thompson		Joseph Bell	Whales – 3 Seals - 17
1790	*Precedent*		Joseph Benn	Whales – 2 Seals – 162 Bears – 3
	Thompson		Joseph Bell	Whales – 2 (lost) Ship lost in the Greenland Sea, 2 June 1790. Crew returned to Leith.
1791	*Precedent*		Captain Wise	Seals – 25 Ship lost off the coast of Ireland, Nov. 1791.

Figure 3.4. Summary of the whaling activity of Whitehaven-built ships, 1762-1791

For three seasons *Thompson* had limited success hunting for whales in the Greenland Sea to the east of Greenland. In 1787 she caught one whale, in 1788 four whales, 28 seals, four unicorns (narwhal) and two bears, and in 1789 three whales and 17 seals. It was not unusual for the owners to engage in other voyages during the early part of the winter as whaleships returned from the Northern Whale Fishery in the autumn and would not have set out again until the following spring. During the autumn of 1787 *Thompson* sailed regularly to Dublin, possibly as a collier.

The 1790 season was more difficult. In July the *Cumberland Pacquet* reported that 'the quantity of ice on the coast...has been much greater than ever was known. The season for seal fishing has been very unsuccessful...we are sorry to add that the scarcity of fish is very much complained of.' The paper went on to report that 'The *Thompson*, Bell, was totally lost on the ice, in the Greenland seas, the second of last month [June]. All the people were saved, and landed at Leith last week, in a vessel belonging to that port. The *Thompson* had got two fish.' As whaling ships usually hunted within sight of other vessels, ship-wrecked crews were normally rescued, although their catch was lost. The ships that brought them home would have been overcrowded with up to double the usual number of crew, and food would probably have been in short supply.

Precedent was the most successful of the Whitehaven whalers although she may only have made a profit in 1789. She sailed on her first voyage in March 1787, with Captain Benn, probably the Captain Joseph Benn of the Whitehaven district of Ginns, as master, and put in at Belfast before sailing north. Like *Thompson* she operated in the Greenland Sea. Once on the whaling grounds she caught six whales and three seals which produced a total of 21.5 tons of blubber. The largest of the whales was 46 feet long with a girth of 24 feet. After being struck by the harpoon this whale had dived below an ice floe, and eleven lines of rope, a total of about one and a half miles, had

Figure 3.5. Daniel Brocklebank's residence in Roper Street, Whitehaven *(photograph: Rob David)*

Figure 3.6. Advertisement in the *Cumberland Pacquet* for the sale of whale oil, September 1787.

to be run out before she surfaced again. The skin of a polar bear was also brought back. This and the 'horn of the Sea Unicorn' (a narwhal) could later be viewed at Crosthwaite's Museum in Keswick, where in 1826 they were described as having been presented by the owners of the 'President [Precedent?] of Whitehaven' (Figure 7.3). Within a few weeks of her return on 8 August, Daniel Brocklebank was advertising 'A quantity of Whale Oil' for sale from his Roper Street premises (Figures 3.5 and 3.6). Like *Thompson, Precedent* was engaged in coastal trade during the autumn, in her case operating between Whitehaven and Waterford.

Between them, *Precedent* and *Thompson* had returned with 38 tons of blubber in 1787, and most of it was presumably purchased by the harbour commissioners for street lighting. As there was still no permanent facility for boiling the oil at the port, the *Cumberland Pacquet* reported that a temporary facility was 'prepared for the purpose on the shore near Parton' (Figure 3.7). The conversion of blubber to whale oil did not require sophisticated equipment. The task could be completed in three or four hours of boiling in large cauldrons and 38 tons could be processed in a day or two. Whalebone (baleen) from the Whitehaven ships would have been bought by local stay manufacturers such as Rose Ingram who advertised her wares in the local press.

In 1788 *Precedent* netted two whales, 'one of them large', one unicorn (narwhal), 17 seals and four seahorses (walruses). 1789 was such a successful season that *Precedent* returned in July. She had caught ten whales and 832 seals. When she returned she also had on board part of the crews of two

Figure 3.7. The beach at Parton *(photograph: Rob David)*

vessels lost in the ice. Her early return enabled her later in the year to sail to Sheepscutt in New England, the location of Daniel Brocklebank's shipyard before the onset of the American War of Independence. She returned in time to set out again 'for the Whale Fishery of the Greenland Seas' in March 1790. After her return on 7 August with two whales, 162 seals and three bears, she sailed to Cork on a number of voyages, finally returning to Whitehaven in January 1791.

Her final voyage to the Greenland Fishery was in 1791 with Captain Wise in command, when she failed to catch any whales and returned with 25 seals only. Her lack of success may reflect the change of master as a successful outcome to a whaling season was very dependent on the skills of the master and the other specialists on board. Over the previous years Captain Benn had shown himself to be a very successful master. Captain Wise seems to have been not so experienced and at the end of the year it was reported that the ship 'is on shore at Wicklow Bank. The people are all saved and it is hoped the vessel will be got off again'. It appears that that hope was not realised. No further ships sailed from Whitehaven to the Northern Whale Fishery.

However, there appears to have been one further eighteenth-century voyage of a Whitehaven-built ship to the Northern Whale Fishery, but on this occasion she sailed from the port of Liverpool. *Venus* had been built at Whitehaven in 1782 for the trans-Atlantic trade and at about 254 tons, she was also of a suitable size for whaling. Her maiden voyage was advertised in the *Cumberland Pacquet* in the spring of 1782, but it seems that the original intention of sailing for Jamaica was not realised, as in April of that year she sailed to Quebec. She remained registered at Whitehaven until 1793 when she was sold to a Mr. Drinkwater at Liverpool. According to Lloyd's Register there was an intention to sail for Greenland in 1797. Neither the owner nor the master W. Hawkins appear elsewhere in the Register with a connection to whaling, so if this voyage actually took place, it is probably an example of a one-off speculative venture which was unsuccessful and therefore not repeated.

THE DEMISE OF WHITEHAVEN AS A WHALING PORT

By 1791 the economic advantages to be derived from involvement in the Northern Whale Fishery were less clear, as the expansion of the national fleet in the late 1780s had created a glut of oil with the price dropping from £28 per tun in 1781 to £17 per tun in 1788.

For Whitehaven engagement in the Northern Whale Fishery was only attractive when the port was suffering an economic slowdown. The whaling trade could not be considered as anything more than a short-term speculative venture encouraged by the existence of the government bounty which in effect underwrote each voyage. It has been calculated that during the 1780s a whaling voyage only became profitable if a ship returned with at least 30 tons of oil and 1½ tons of bone, so it is possible that *Precedent*'s voyage in 1789 was the only profitable one made from Whitehaven. The loss of the tobacco trade to Glasgow during the 1750s and some of the coal trade to neighbouring ports from the late 1780s resulted in Whitehaven shipowners and merchants searching for new opportunities, and their participation in whaling should probably be viewed alongside their interest in the slave trade. However, in both cases the shipowners and masters suffered from a lack of expertise in sailing conditions along the coasts and in the seas that the ships visited. Their lack of knowledge of the African coast and of the slave trade in comparison with their competitors from rival ports meant that they were placed at an immediate disadvantage. The same would have been true of Arctic conditions and limited expertise in the non-traditional trade of whaling. The remoteness of Whitehaven and the restricted local market created difficulties both for whalers and slave traders. The owners of whaleships faced what would prove to be insurmountable further problems. These included reductions in the bounty to 25*s.* per ton in 1793, and to 20*s.* in 1796, the continuing lack of investment in whaling infrastructure at the port, and the outbreak of the French wars in 1793. Despite some expansion of the market, there was little incentive for Whitehaven shipowners, like those at other small west-coast ports, to continue whaling. The lack of investment in infrastructure also made it easy for Whitehaven to abandon whaling when economic conditions changed or war intervened.

In 1809, *Alfred*, a ship built at Whitehaven in 1796, was sold to Hull and converted to a whaleship. News of this development may have prompted the Whitehaven harbour trustees to hope for a revival in the whaling industry as, in an Act of Parliament of 1816, they were permitted to levy a duty of 1*s*. 6*d*. per ton on vessels entering the harbour from 'Greenland, or Davies's Streights', and the collection of 2*d*. per cwt. on whalebone, and 8*d*. per 100 gallons on whale or train oil. Although whaling revived nationally in the years following the defeat of Napoleon, the industry was centred on the east-coast ports where expertise resided and the refining infrastructure existed, and ports such as Whitehaven, Greenock, Liverpool, Bristol and Exeter no longer participated. But Whitehaven continued to be connected to the industry through ships built in the town sailing to the Northern Whale Fishery from other ports as described in Chapter 4.

★ ★ ★ ★ ★

Suggested Further Reading

T. Barrow, *The Whaling Trade of North-East England 1750-1850*, (Sunderland, University of Sunderland, 2001).

A. C. Credland, *The Hull Whaling Trade: An Arctic Enterprise*, (Beverley, Hutton Press, 1995).

R. David, 'Whitehaven and the Northern Whale Fishery', *Northern History*, xlvii:1, March 2010, 117-134.

R. David, ' "A Perilous Situation": Whitehaven-built ships in the Northern Whale Fishery', *Transactions of the Cumberland and Westmorland Antiquarian and Archaeological Society*, Third Series, Vol. X, 2010, 197-216.

P. Hoare, *Leviathan or, The Whale*, (London, Harper Collins, 2008).

G. Jackson, *The British Whaling Trade*, (London, A&C Black, 1978; [reprinted in *Research in Maritime History*, No.29, 2005]).

B. Lubbock, *The Arctic Whalers*, (Glasgow, Brown, Son and Ferguson, 1937 [reprint 1978]).

W.G. Ross, *Arctic Whalers, Icy Seas: Narratives of the Davis Strait Whale Fishery*, (Toronto, Irwin, 1985).

Chapter 4

'Ships that have left their bones in the battlefield of Melville Bay': The Arctic voyages of *Alfred* and *Jumna*, 1809-1863

After Whitehaven ceased its direct involvement in Arctic whaling, its shipyards continued to build ships for the West India trade, and a few which were destined to become East Indiamen. Two of these vessels were subsequently converted into whaling ships and sailed annually to the Arctic before succumbing to the dangers of that region and being crushed by ice.

Figure 4.1. Whitehaven harbour. Drawn and engraved by William Daniell, 1816 *(reproduced by courtesy of Cumbria County Council, Carlisle Library)*

The whale ship *Alfred*

The 314 tons, three-masted, square-rigged ship, *Alfred* was constructed in Whitehaven (Figure 4.1) in 1796 at the Bransty shipyard founded by Daniel Brocklebank but by then under the control of Thomas and John Brocklebank. She transferred to Liverpool and between 1797 and 1800 sailed from that port to various islands in the West Indies. Daniel Brocklebank's son, Daniel junior, was captain but died of yellow fever at Montego Bay in Jamaica in 1798. On the outward voyage *Alfred* would no doubt have carried Lancashire-made manufactured goods, whereas inbound her holds would have been full of goods such as mahogany, cotton, indigo, sugar and coffee. In 1800 she was sold to a Lancaster company and continued to sail from there to the West Indies until at least 1802 (Figure 4.2). Between 1802 and 1809 her movements are uncertain, but on 29 May 1809 her registration at the whaling port of Hull signalled a new use. She was reported as sailing from London to Hull in March 1810 under the command of John Dick, so it is possible that the necessary refit which would enable her to sail in Arctic waters had taken place in London. Initially ownership was invested in three members of a Hull merchant family, the Halls, but over the next few years ownership was as usual spread more widely. The Hall family kept their interest, but their new co-owners included other merchants from Hull, Whitby and elsewhere in Yorkshire. For the next 27 seasons she sailed in almost every year from Hull to the Northern Whale Fishery.

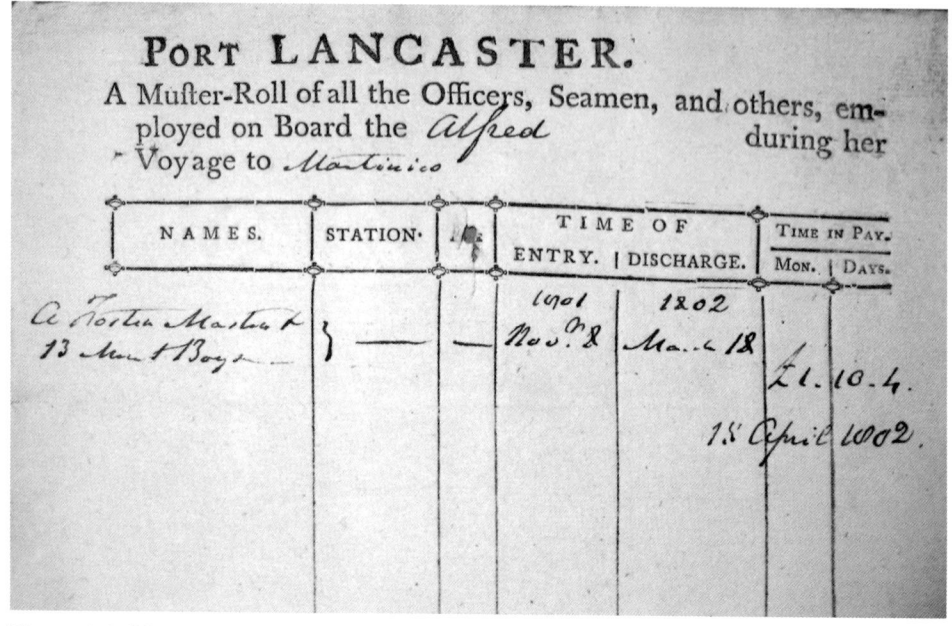

Figure 4.2. Muster Roll for *Alfred* sailing from Lancaster to Martinico 1801-2 *(reproduced by courtesy of the National Archives, London)*

John Dick was master between 1810 and 1815, a period during which *Alfred* was one of Hull's more successful whalers. Inevitably catches varied from season to season, for example, a single whale in 1813 and 14 whales the following year. Dick was followed for four seasons by Martin Morris during whose time 15 whales were killed along with 110 seals. Seals were taken early in the season, and seal oil could be a useful supplement to whale oil, especially in lean whaling years. In 1820 William Clark became master for two years. Although he was successful in his first year, returning with the products of five whales, in the following season *Alfred* returned to Hull 'clean', which meant that she had failed to catch any whales (Figure 4.3). When this happened the company would suffer financial hardship and the crew would be impoverished, since they would have had to rely solely on their wages as they would have earned no 'whale oil' bonus. This lack of success probably contributed to the ship being laid up in 1822-24 and then being sold to the leading Hull merchants, Gardiner and Joseph Egginton, who once again fitted her out for the Northern Whale Fishery in 1825. For the next twelve years she sailed from Hull annually as part of their fleet of up to sixteen whaling vessels.

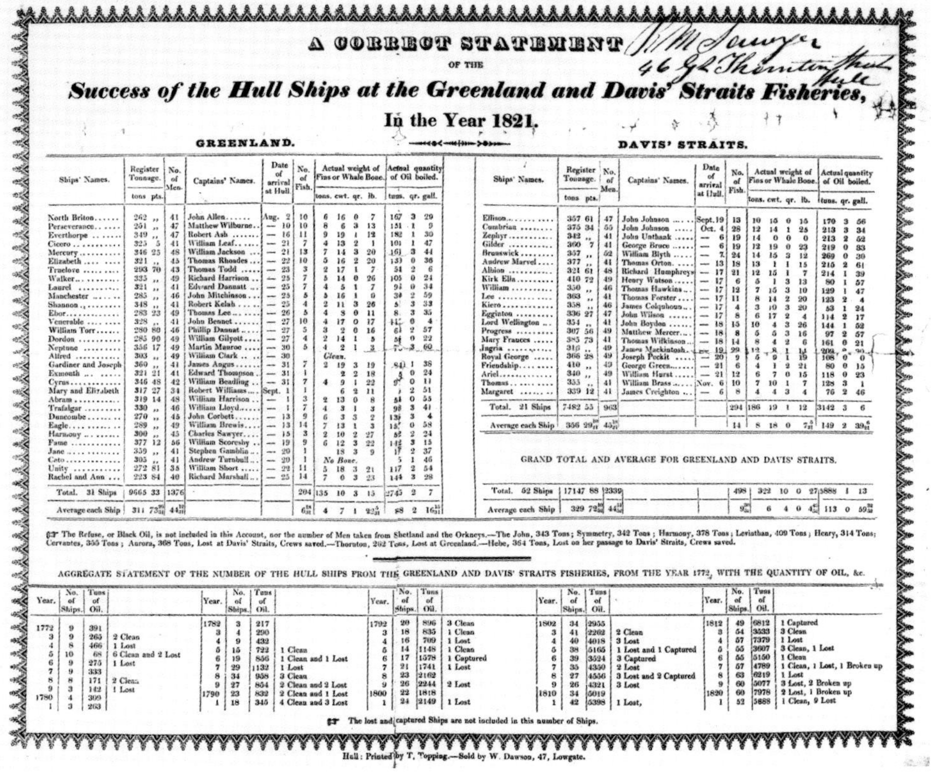

Figure 4.3. List of whaling vessels sailing from Hull to the Northern Whale Fishery in 1821 (© *Hull Maritime Museums: Hull Museums*)

During these years *Alfred* caught 101 whales and returned with almost 325,000 gallons of oil. She was one of the most successful vessels in the British fleet at a time when whaling became a much more uncertain industry. Whales were becoming scarcer in the traditional fishing areas of the Greenland Sea and Davis Strait, so the fleet had to sail further north and west in Baffin Bay towards more dangerous and uncharted waters, which extended the period away from the home port towards the start of winter. The Eggintons employed three masters between 1825 and 1835. In 1827 John Martin, the second of their whaling masters, was particularly successful returning to Hull with nearly 50,000 gallons of oil, the produce of twenty whales. This was the best year enjoyed by *Alfred*.

William Brass was master between 1830 and 1835. These years were amongst the most dramatic in Arctic whaling history. The 1830 season was the worst ever experienced by the whaling fleet. It was unusually cold and stormy, and of the 91 British ships in Davis Strait during that season, 19 were lost and 21 returned 'clean'. Nearly 20% of the Hull fleet was wrecked that year, and those ships that returned, which included *Alfred*, only caught 77 whales between them. *Alfred* was one of the most successful of the Hull ships returning with five whales and over 20,000 gallons of oil, as well as four tons of whalebone. The resulting shortage of whale oil nationally caused the price to rise to £60 per ton, a boon for those ships that had been successful and a further impetus for those industries that used whale oil to continue their search for substitutes.

There was a decline in the size of the British whaling fleet in 1832 and 1833, but those ships which persevered, including *Alfred*, had profitable seasons. In both years *Alfred* returned to Hull with the products of twenty whales, although they must have been smaller than those caught in 1827 as less whale oil was produced. The fact that smaller whales were being caught was symptomatic of the overfishing that was already beginning to affect the newer fishing grounds. 1835 was another disastrous year for the whaling fleet. As winter approached eleven British ships became trapped in the ice in the western Davis Strait. *Alfred* was frozen in for a few days, but she was able to make her escape in October and returned to Hull on 12th November, with an additional eight crew members from the wrecked *Mary Frances* on board. William Brass brought the first news of the fleet's predicament, and on instructions from the Hull ship owners and the Admiralty, was called to a meeting in Hull to give his advice as to what action might be taken. It was decided that the eminent Arctic navigator and explorer, Captain James Clark Ross R. N., should lead a rescue mission to Davis Strait, but before any rescue ships could be sent to the area all but one of those beset in the ice escaped when the southward drift of the ice caused it to melt as it reached more temperate waters and enabled the ships to return to the United Kingdom. One ship was lost with all hands, and the condition of many of the sailors who returned was so pitiable, that those with the worst cases of scurvy were disembarked at Stromness in Orkney. The events of that winter resulted in a much reduced fleet in 1836. *Alfred* did sail that year, but on her return she was put up for sale and purchased by John Anderson, an owner of whaling vessels and boiling houses in Bo'ness on the Firth of Forth.

Bo'ness was one of a number of Scottish east-coast whaling ports which were involved intermittently with the Northern Whale Fishery. John Anderson not only owned some whaling vessels but also the boiling houses with their huge copper pans in which the blubber was rendered into oil. The landing of whale blubber and the making of whale oil were filthy activities supervised by the harpooners and undertaken by the whaling crews during the winter. In 1830 the little seaside resort of Burntisland in Fife, a few miles from Bo'ness, was threatened with a whale oil factory, and those who opposed such a development did not exaggerate when they wrote that:

> the blubber, when moved, gets into a state of fermentation, often bursting the casks, or throwing out the bungs, and dispersing their contents in the ship, or during the removal to the storehouses or boiling places. The sickening fumes all the while are widely diffused, even to the distance of miles. The nuisance does not cease with the act of boiling, which may terminate in six or eight weeks...Not only are the ships themselves in a disgusting state, but the empty blubber casks, and whalebone, or gills, which are stored up in great quantity, and often kept in that state many months, become extremely rancid and offensive; not to mention the refuse from the boilers, which is so highly putrid, and unconquerably bad, that the mere sprinkling or droppings from the carts employed to remove it, pollute the roads and streets through which they pass to such a degree, that they are frequently not purified or divested of the smell for weeks afterwards.

Like most of the whaling fleet, *Alfred* would have left Bo'ness in the spring, accompanied by the usual noisy send-off by loved ones and well-wishers, and bound for Lerwick in the Shetland Islands. Lerwick was the last port of call before the whalers set sail for the Arctic, so it was an opportunity for the ship's company to purchase supplies for the whaling season, and for the master to complete his crew with the skilled oarsmen that lived on these northern islands. There were a number of ship chandlers at Lerwick who acted as agents for the whaling companies, and one of these was Hay and Company. This company became involved in the whaling trade in 1844, and *Alfred* was the third vessel on its books in 1845 when she sailed from Bo'ness as part of John Anderson's fleet. In 1846, for example, the records show that on arrival at Lerwick *Alfred* engaged 27 Shetlanders, one of whom was William Williamson. On March 24 1846 he purchased from Hay's two pairs of drawers, one pair of canvas trousers, one pair of breeches, two shirts, a nightcap, duck cloth, sheets, handkerchiefs and three pairs of mittens. Sailors were responsible for their own clothing, and the fact that he needed all this, despite having sailed in *Alfred* the previous year, shows the wear and tear on clothing caused by working on a whale ship, and also perhaps the all-pervading smell which could never be washed out of cloth. He also bought oatmeal, coffee and sugar, presumably to supplement the food provided on board by the ship's cook, and purchased a tin basin, a towel, soap, tobacco and a share in a frying pan. In addition he borrowed cash to the sum of £1 5s 6d. His credit totalled £3 7s 10d. It is likely that most of these items were for the voyage, but some purchases may have been made on behalf of his family. His family bought more items while he was at sea:- tea, oatmeal, India meal, bymeal, bread, a bottle of rum, soap, linen and frocks, as well as taking out some more cash and paying into the seaman fund (an insurance against unexpected expenditure or loss of earnings), and paying for the carting of peat for their winter fire. Williamson earned £10 14s 0d for a voyage lasting seven months and four days, as well as a bonus of £3 15s 0d for his proportion of the sixty tons of oil money. At the end of this season his family's income and expenditure approximately balanced, but after a poor whaling season many would have been very impoverished, especially if they were unable to find work over the winter.

We know little of the events that took place during her voyages from Bo'ness. In 1845, as in most years, some of *Alfred*'s crew were on their first voyage which meant that they had to endure the traditions of the Neptune festival on 1 May. The famous Whitby whaling captain, William Scoresby, had described what happened on this day in his *Journal of a Voyage to the Northern Whale Fishery*, published in 1822:

> The 1st day of May is usually ushered in by the Greenland sailors, by the suspension in the rigging of a garland of ribbons, attended with grotesque dances and other amusements, and occasionally with ceremonies somewhat similar to those commonly practised in crossing the line. One at a time they [those on their first voyage] were brought into Neptune's presence, and each submitted to his humorous interrogatories, and to the coarse operation of shaving.

In 1842 Thomas Grant, then aged eleven, had approached Captain Walker, the master of *Alfred*, to be an apprentice but had been turned down. However, he was not to be put off, and threatening to go 'in spite of him', had hidden on board the ship before it set sail. He later reported:

> I boarded his ship and stowed myself away under some straw, which had been brought on board with some potatoes and had

been placed in the seamen's bunks. As the vessel got to sea, I became rather uneasy in my confinement and this led to my discovery by two sailors who occupied these bunks. In the morning I was taken before the skipper [who was] rather tickled at my boldness in having carried out my threat. The Alfred was a little square-rigged ship and he ordered me to go aloft and loosen the top-gallant sail. I went aloft and after a little guidance from the skipper, managed to do so. These operations of mine were keenly watched not only by the skipper but my father, who was the harpooner on board but who, until then, was quite unaware of my bold venture. The skipper handed me over to him, with the instruction to make me a half-deck boy. The duty of such was to carry the food of the harpooners from the galley to the half-deck and make myself generally useful on board. We went to Greenland and returned with seven whales.

In 1847 *Alfred* sailed on her final voyage to the whale fishery. As usual she called in at Lerwick and the Hay and Company ledger records purchases by 'The Shetlandmen on board the Alfred', 'Captain John Isles of the Alfred', and on behalf of 'ship Alfred' (Figure 4.4). We know little about the voyage, beyond the fact that she had only caught a single whale, before the events of 3 July when she was crushed by the ice in Davis Strait. Amongst the crew was the stowaway Thomas Grant, by then employed as an apprentice. Her destruction was witnessed by Mr. F. Lee, the mate on *Bon Accord* of Hull. He reported the events in a letter to his wife which was printed at length in numerous contemporary newspapers. He wrote that *Alfred* sank in the early hours of 3 July 1847 at 75°N. At the time 'it was blowing a hurricane from the SW with constant snow'. The ice was on the move and 'the Alfred was about 200 yards ahead...she took the first nip and the ice went right over her'. She sank a short time later. Subsequently the *Bon Accord* also sank. Both crews were saved but had to camp on the ice. The *Alfred's* crew 'were a great deal more comfortable, for they had saved their bed clothes and their chests all dry'. Between them the two ships had managed to save seven of their whale boats which enabled the two ships' companies to consider rescuing themselves by rowing towards the nearest settlement on the Greenland coast. Each of the whale boats would have to accommodate three times their normal crew. The weather remained stormy the following day, but on 5 July it was calm and warm.

At this point Thomas Grant takes up the story:

> There were seven small boats in all, each containing fifteen hands, with provisions and clothing recovered from the wrecks. When the wind permitted we hoisted sail and made good progress. Left

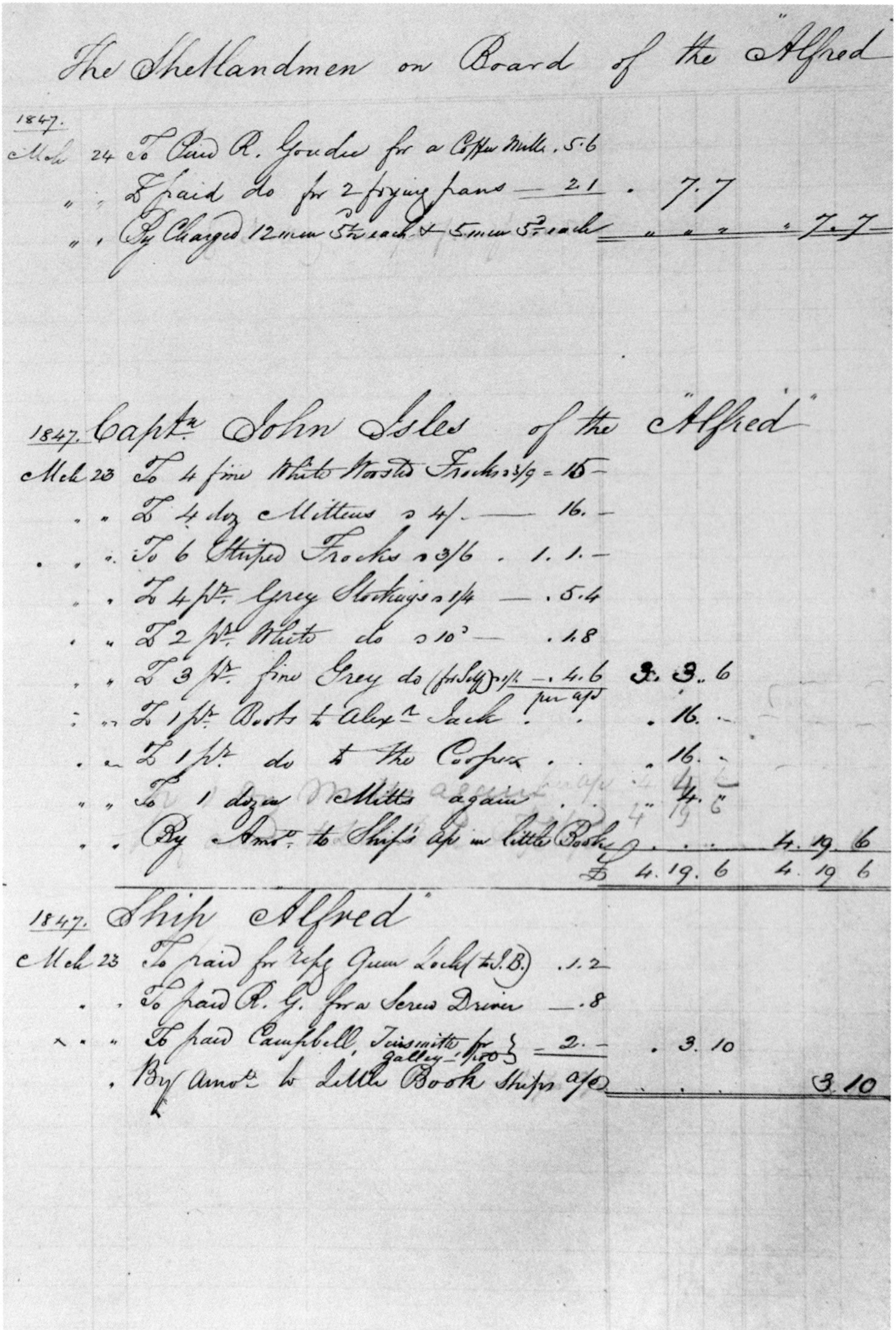
The Shetlandmen on Board of the "Alfred"
1847.
Mch 24 To Paid R. Goudie for a Coffee Mill . 5.6
" " To paid do for 2 frying pans — 2.1 . 7.7
" " By Charged 12 men 5½ each & 5 men 5⅔ each . . . 7.7

1847. Captn John Isles of the "Alfred"
Mch 23 To 4 fine White Worsted Frocks 3/9 = 15 —
" " To 4 doz Mittens 4/ — 16. —
" " To 6 Striped Frocks 3/6 . 1. 1. —
" " To 4 prs Grey Stockings 1/4 — . 5.4
" " To 2 prs White do 10d — . 1.8
" " To 3 prs fine Grey do (for Self) 1/6 — . 4.6 3. 3. 6
" " To 1 pr Boots to Alexr Jack per a/c . 16. —
" " To 1 pr do to the Cooper . 16. —
" " To 1 dozen Mitts again 4.6
" " By Amt to Ship's a/c in little Book . . . 4.19.6
£ 4.19.6 4.19.6

1847. Ship "Alfred"
Mch 23 To paid for repg Gun Lock (to J.B.) . 1.2
" " To paid R. G. for a Screw Driver — . 8
" " To paid Campbell Tinsmith for galley-pipe 2. — . 3.10
" By Amt to Little Book Ships a/c . . . 3.10

Figure 4.4. The purchases by crew members of *Alfred* as recorded in the Hay and Company ledger, 1847. Shetland Archives D31/6 *(reproduced by courtesy of Shetland Archives)* without wind, we plied the oars and covered close on 600 miles. We landed ultimately at Leevely [Godhavn on Disco Island], a Danish settlement and were taken on board a Danish brig, *Lousinda* of Copenhagen. She took us to the Shetland Islands and there transferred us to an English schooner, which landed us in Aberdeen. We then took steamer for Granton and as distressed seamen, our passages were paid by the Fisherman's Society and the Sea-Box Society.

Some other members of *Alfred*'s crew reached Britain via Copenhagen and Hamburg. As was usual the entire ship's company had been saved. *Alfred* had successfully fished in Arctic waters for the best part of 37 years - testament to the shipbuilding skills of those at Whitehaven who had built her 51 years earlier.

THE WHALE SHIP *JUMNA*

Jumna was the last of the Whitehaven ships which were later refitted as whalers. Like *Alfred* she was a three-masted, square-rigged, wooden sailing ship built at the Brocklebank shipyard (Figure 4.5). She was built in 1833, 37 years after *Alfred*, and cost £7,118. At 364 tons and with a length of 107'10", a beam of 27'9" and draught of 18'11", she was one of the largest ships constructed in this shipyard. She joined the Brocklebank fleet at Liverpool and remained with the company until she was sold in 1856. This was a period of rapid expansion during which Brocklebanks capitalised on trading opportunities in India and, to a lesser extent, in China. By 1844 the Brocklebank fleet numbered some fifty vessels. However, by the mid-1850s the company was contracting and in 1856 *Jumna* was sold to the Tay Whale Fishing Company of Dundee, where she was re-registered as a whaler the following year, and sailed to Davis Strait and Baffin Bay between 1858 and 1863, before suffering a similar fate to *Alfred* by being crushed by ice in Melville Bay.

In the mid-1830s *Jumna* was the fastest ship sailing to India and China. Her maiden voyage from Liverpool to Calcutta and back was completed in the then record time of eight months and two days. According to a contemporary Whitehaven newspaper, the passengers travelled in some style and comfort: 'Accommodation for passengers is admirable both in size and finish of the berths and state cabins'. Her second voyage was to Canton. After 212 days at sea she returned to Liverpool with over 6000 packages of tea, along with silk, ivory, fans and preserves. *Gore's Liverpool Advertiser* noted: 'This we believe the quickest voyage to China and back ever known. The *Jumna* is the first ship that has made the voyage between this port and Canton direct'. Apart from a single further voyage to Canton in 1835, all subsequent voyages, prior to her sale to Dundee, were made from Liverpool to Calcutta.

Figure 4.5. Whitehaven from Bransty Hill. Drawn and engraved by W. Westall c1830 *(reproduced by courtesy of Cumbria County Council, Carlisle Library)*

During the 1850s Dundee's need for whale oil increased as the jute industry expanded. Indian jute was used for sacking, carpetbacking and linoleum, and whale oil was the most suitable material for softening the fibres before spinning. The newly formed Tay Whale Fishing Company sought to capitalise on the development of this industry and the purchase of *Jumna* was part of the firm's expansion. At that time the Dundee shipyards were experimenting with converting old wooden whaling ships from sail to steam power but initially *Jumna* continued as a sailing vessel. After the usual refit she was re-registered at Dundee on 15 January 1857.

She sailed to Davis Strait in the same year under the command of Captain Alexander Deuchars. Deuchars, a native of Dundee, was aged 49 years and had previously captained *Princess Charlotte* which he lost in June 1856. In 1857 *Jumna* returned to Dundee with the produce of four whales amounting to 58 tuns of oil and 3.5 tons of whale bone. In the following year she departed from Dundee on 17 March 1858, under the command of George Deuchars, also of Dundee. The ship's company of 49 all signed on in Dundee. Of the 49, 63% had been born in Dundee, and most of the remainder came from various ports along the east coast of Scotland. The average age was 29.5, with actual ages ranging from 65 (the cook) to 17 (an apprentice). Only nine sailors did not have the necessary level of literacy to sign their own name. After putting in at Stromness on Orkney for final supplies the *Jumna* continued directly to Davis Strait. The voyage seems to have been uneventful and resulted in three whales being caught. These produced 45 tuns of oil. The only untoward event occurred on 24 August when the carpenter, Alexander Anderson, refused to do any more work. He apparently armed himself with an axe, but was overpowered and put in irons. He was released the next day and ordered by the master to return to work. He said that he would think about it, but he seems to have chosen not to, although he behaved himself for the rest of the voyage. Consequently he forfeited all further pay.

In 1859 and 1860 Captain Alexander Stuart of Peterhead commanded the ship on voyages to Davis Strait. In 1859 two whales were caught (25 tuns of oil) and in 1860, three whales (40 tuns of oil). *Jumna*'s voyage to Davis Strait in 1859 followed the traditional practice of calling in at Lerwick, where twelve Shetlanders joined the ship's company. Hay and Company acted as the agents for the Tay Whale Fishing Company as they had for *Alfred* earlier. As well as the Shetlanders purchasing their personal requirements from the company, the Dundee men also bought their final purchases for the voyage. Hay's supplied them with 'hosiery', a mixture of mittens, souwesters, oiled trousers, trousers, braces, sailing caps, night caps, canvas trousers, oiled jackets, stockings, canvas, white and blue frocks, gloves, drawers, caps as well as a cravat and a small shawl. They also purchased coffee, a coffee mill, mustard, pepper, combs, knives, frying pans and a kettle. In total they bought £17 6s 10d worth of goods. Captain Stuart purchased a souwester, gloves, three dozen mittens, two Shetland night caps, a bag and six pairs of stockings on his own account (£1 18s 8d), and eighty dried eggs, two frying pans and a coffee mill on the ship's account.

Jumna's most successful voyage was in 1861 when, once again under the command of Alexander Deuchars, she returned from the western side of Davis Strait with eighteen whales and 140 tuns of oil. Deuchars had gained further experience between 1858 and 1860, first as master of *Tay* and then of *Dundee*. His skill will almost certainly have contributed to *Jumna*'s success, although it has to be said that 1861 was a very good year for the Dundee whalers. *Narwhal*, for example, caught 29 whales and *Wildfire*, 21. Deuchars remained master in both 1862 and 1863 when *Jumna* was at the centre of a series of disasters that beset the whaling fleet. The events of those years were published at length in newspapers across the country, so consequently there is a clear picture of her role in the dramatic events which were taking place in Davis Strait.

The events of 1862 were reported by Captain Wells, master of *Emma* of Hull. Like *Jumna*, *Emma* was a sailing vessel and was trapped, along with *Jumna* and much of the rest of the fleet, by 'a heavy barrier of ice' which prevented the ships from reaching Melville Bay on the west coast of Greenland for most of June and July. Eventually on the 16 July the fleet was able to sail through a series of leads in the ice into Melville Bay, but a change of wind direction the following day put the ships into great danger. The words of Captain Wells provide a vivid description of the events of the following weeks:

> On the 17th July the ships sped northward through very narrow and intricate channels of water, and great hopes were entertained of getting into the north waters, and thence to the west side of the Straits, but to our great disappointment the weather became deadly thick, with snow and fog, and we soon found ourselves embayed in the ice, which was closing so rapidly that no time was to be lost in getting the ship into a safe position. All hands were called ... and a dock was cut in the land ice, which was much thicker than we had ever before known it, averaging about seven feet. The docks took eleven hours to cut, and the ships were only got in in time to save them from damage, as other floes were closing in rapidly and causing great pressure…. Our position

in the bay was anything but enviable, as we lay at the foot of the great ice glacier which forms the arm or throat of the bay. The icebergs around were immensely large and innumerable. The floes, or sheets of flat ice, were also exceedingly heavy and dangerous. On the night of the 27th there were evident signs of an approaching storm, which made us feel very uneasy for the safety of the ships. On the following morning the hurricane reached us, accompanied with rain and snow, and never in my experience have I seen such a dreadful storm in these high latitudes. ... Boats, provisions, bags of clothes, beds etc were taken out of the ships to temporary canvas tents on the ice, the ships being in such a perilous situation that it was at one time thought that not one out of the twelve in company would be saved to carry home the 600 who were standing on the ice watching their fate. During the night the gale continued to rage with great fury, and the pressure amongst the ice in some places was so great that in the neighbourhood where the *Jumna*, of Dundee, and the *Active* of Peterhead, lay docked, it was observed that the floes run over the tops of icebergs sixty feet high, and fell down with a tremendous crash on the other side, close to the ships.

At this point *Abram* of Kirkcaldy, a Lancaster-built ship, 'was crushed to atoms' and *Alexander* of Dundee 'also went to pieces':

Consternation ran through the whole fleet, and it was truly distressing to see the wretched men dragging the few clothes they had saved along the ice to the other ships. The crews of the yet surviving ships wandered about in the rain and snow, with their beds and clothes saturated with wet. ... When the gale abated rain, snow and sleet began to fall in torrents, until the decks of the ships were completely flooded. The following day, on looking from the masthead, not a drop of water could be seen. The ice was crushed up and overlapped in some places three or four feet thick.

By August, the summer was far advanced and night frosts were causing the ice to thicken. There seemed to be no way of escape:

After lying a week in this miserable position... [the ships' companies including those of] the *Jumna* and *Active* commenced sawing...from the nearest lane of water to where the ships lay. The sky again blackened and another heavy southerly gale approaching, made what preparation was necessary, and in a few hours it was raging with dreadful fury. The icebergs again began their work of destruction; the ice that had been fast to the land now became torn into parts, and the ships began to drive to the north along with it. All our clothes, beds, provisions etc, were again put on the ice, and for about 48 hours we scarcely knew from one hour to another whether our ship would weather the storm.

On this occasion the ten ships survived, but with the crews of the two wrecked ships divided between the surviving ships, conditions were cramped and rations in short supply. The remaining ships were still iced in on the 20th August and the crews were put on 'short allowance and the fires were put out after cooking'. However, warmer weather put the ice in motion and on the 23rd all but one of the ships, thanks in large part to the efforts of *Jumna*'s crew, escaped into open water. During the previous six weeks the almost constant southerly wind had caused the ships to drift further north, almost to Cape York at the northern end of Melville Bay. Captain Wells had nothing but praise for the crew of *Jumna*:

> The crews of *Jumna* and *Active*, in getting out of the ice, had accomplished a feat that I fear not to say had never been done in this country, a description of which could scarcely be credited, having made a way for seven or eight miles through very heavy ice by means of warping, sawing and blasting.

22 of the 49 strong crew had sailed with Captain Deuchars in 1861 and the loyalty to their master that this suggests will have helped the crew survive the dangers. Having escaped the ice in Melville Bay the fleet did not return home but continued to their original destination, the Baffin Island coast to the west of Davis Strait. *Jumna* eventually returned to Dundee on 8 October.

1862 was a particularly bad year, especially for Dundee's neighbouring port of Kirkcaldy whose entire whaling fleet sank in Melville Bay. That year the steamships, with their extra power, were able to pass through the ice to the 'North Water' and the western coast of Baffin Bay without the problems that had confronted the sailing vessels. The Dundee ship owners were becoming convinced of the advantages of converting their wooden sailing vessels to steam power, while maintaining adequate sail coverage to enable them to reduce costs through using wind power whenever possible. By keeping sails in reserve, it also allowed the ships to operate silently when in whaling waters. *Jumna* was one of the sailing ships converted to steam power during the winter of 1862-63.

With Captain Deuchars once again master, *Jumna* sailed for Davis Strait on 19 March 1863. On this occasion the crew numbered 51 and included for the first time an engineer and two firemen. Nearly half the crew consisted of returnees from the 1862 voyage. Sailing past Orkney and Shetland, she entered Davis Strait on 27 May 'having made bad passage'. The ice conditions proved as taxing as in the previous year. Captain Wells of *Lady Seale* and Captain Walker of *Wildfire* provided a commentary on the events as they unfolded. By the last week in June, seven steamships, including *Jumna*, entered Melville Bay. Progress north was maintained until the 2nd July:

> Here we were brought to a standstill – in fact, put to our wits' end. We could neither advance nor retreat. The ice in this place was very thick, the single ice being from seven to ten feet, and in some places along the edge of the floe it was squeezed to sixty or seventy feet in thickness. ... I have been on a lee shore more than once, and have seen death staring me in the face...and here we had to stand with our hands in our pockets; could do nothing but look on, expecting every minute to see our great ships made mincemeat of. On the 6th the ice began to move slowly, and ...a sudden and fearfully tremendous rush took place, crushing in the whole starboard broadside as if the ship [*Lady Seale*] had been an egg-shell, when she began immediately to fill and settle down. The boats with the crew were got away at all possible speed – every one working with a will, life itself now being wholly dependent on each man's activity. Louder than the wind, and the bustle of 300 men trying to save their boats and a few things, was heard the breaking of bolts and the tearing to pieces of the good old oak. The ice at the time took full charge of all the ships now lying in close proximity to one another, and the *Jumna* also received a fatal squeeze.

Lady Seale sank within ten minutes, 'her stern foremost, her bowsprit end pointing towards the heavens, as if bidding farewell to the light of day before descending to her future icebound home'. *Jumna* 'also sunk in a very few hours to swell the number of ships that have left their bones in the battlefield of Melville Bay'. The crews of both ships escaped onto the ice, lost the greater part of their clothing, and were divided amongst the remaining ships. On the ice were both Captain Deuchars and David Soutar, the mate on board *Lady Seale*, who had the previous year been the master of the Lancaster-built *Abram*, whose demise had been witnessed by Alexander Deuchars. A month or so later those members of the ship's company that had been taken in by *Tay*, rowed one of the surviving ship's boats to Umanaaq, a trading settlement on an island off the Greenland coast where they were taken on board a Danish schooner bound for Copenhagen. 'After a long and tedious voyage – the crew having no other place to sleep on than amongst the oil casks in the forehold – they were landed at Westray on Orkney', from where they made their way to Kirkwall. The rest of the crew, with the exception of the engineer who died from consumption, eventually returned to Dundee on board the other whalers in the fleet. The loss of *Jumna* meant that Whitehaven's century - long connection with Arctic whaling was brought to an end.

★ ★ ★ ★ ★

SUGGESTED FURTHER READING

T. Barrow, *The Whaling Trade of North-East England 1750-1850*, (Sunderland, University of Sunderland Press, 2001).

A. C. Credland, *The Hull Whaling Trade: An Arctic Enterprise*, (Beverley, Hutton Press, 1995).

R. David, 'Whitehaven and the Northern Whale Fishery', *Northern History*, xlvii: 1, March 2010, 117-134.

R. David, ' "A Perilous Situation": Whitehaven-built ships in the Northern Whale Fishery', *Transactions of the Cumberland and Westmorland Antiquarian and Archaeological Society*, Third Series, Vol. X, 2010, 197-216.

P. Hoare, *Leviathan or, The Whale* (London, Harper Collins, 2008).

D. Hollett, *From Cumberland to Cape Horn: The Sailing Fleet of Thomas and John Brocklebank of Whitehaven and Liverpool 1770-1900* (London, Fairplay, 1984).

G. Jackson, *The British Whaling Trade* (London, A&C Black, 1978; [reprinted in *Research in Maritime History*, No.29, 2005]).

B. Lubbock, *The Arctic Whalers* (Glasgow, Brown, Son and Ferguson, 1937 [reprint 1978]).

W.G. Ross, *Arctic Whalers, Icy Seas: Narratives of the Davis Strait Whale Fishery*, (Toronto, Irwin, 1985).

Chapter 5
'I know it is in existence, and not very hard to find': Searching for the North West Passage, 1818-1859

It was a Cumbrian, Sir John Barrow, who as second secretary to the Admiralty instigated the era of intensive exploration of the Arctic regions to the west of Greenland and to the north of Canada which began in 1818, but none of his naval commanders or senior officers came from the county, and few, if any, of the ships' companies were born there. However, a number of Barrow's men came to have connections to the county. Sir John Richardson retired there, Sir William Edward Parry was painted on the wall of a Cumbrian house, and Parry along with one of the Ross family, Sir John or his nephew Sir James Clark, found themselves inscribed on slate in a quarry on the shore of Lake Windermere. As well as the Admiralty-organised expeditions there were other private expeditions in search of the North West Passage, and some of their ships' companies included sailors born in, or connected, to Cumbria. However, it is Sir John Barrow himself who has the most visible monument to his achievements.

Sir John Barrow (1764-1848) and the Hoad Monument at Ulverston

A great age of polar exploration began with the ending of the Napoleonic wars, and it was Sir John Barrow who was responsible for sending expeditions to search for the North West Passage and also to investigate the region around the North Pole (Figure 5.1). With the ending of war in 1815, Britain had no further need for a navy designed for almost constant warfare. Consequently there were large numbers of ships, many officers of all ranks, and innumerable seamen who were then surplus to requirements. Although seamen were easily laid off, surplus officers still had to be paid, and not all ships could be decommissioned or mothballed. Second Secretary to the Admiralty, Sir John Barrow, saw that this situation provided a unique opportunity for him to indulge his passion for exploration by sending naval vessels and half-pay officers on voyages of exploration, particularly to Africa and the Arctic. Further exploration of the Arctic was considered justifiable as the recent wars had interrupted British exploration of the region, a process that had continued intermittently since the reign of Elizabeth I. It was an area where it was thought that economic and imperial opportunities existed. It was also believed to be in the national interest for Britain to have a navy skilled in Arctic navigation. Barrow was the right person in the right job at the right time to enable the country to take advantage of these opportunities.

Figure 5.1. Portrait of Sir John Barrow by George Thomas Payne, after John Lucas, mezzotint, published 27 May 1847. National Portrait Gallery D19840 (© *National Portrait Gallery, London*)

John Barrow had been born at Dragley Beck, near Ulverston, in 1764 (Figure 5.2) and received what formal education he had at Town Bank School. He left at the age of thirteen, and after a variety of jobs which included serving in a whaling ship in Arctic waters near Spitsbergen, he reached London where he became tutor to Thomas Staunton, the unusually gifted son of Sir George Staunton. While John Barrow tutored the young boy, Thomas taught Barrow to read and write Chinese. Sir George acted as his patron and through his connections arranged for him to join Lord Macartney's embassy to China as his interpreter. When Macartney was later sent to South Africa, Barrow again accompanied him, this time as one of his secretaries. Contacts he made in South Africa enabled him to gain the ear of First Lord of the Admiralty, Lord Melville, who appointed him second secretary of the Admiralty on his return to London in 1804. There were two secretaries who together were the most influential people in the Admiralty – a fact which was reflected in their salaries. As second secretary Barrow was paid as much as the first lord of the Admiralty - £2000 per annum. The first secretary was a politician and responsible for dealing with the political aspects of running the navy. The second secretary 'was responsible for running the Admiralty office and supervising the very extensive correspondence with naval officers all over the world, as well as with agents of other boards'. This was a role that the ambitious Barrow made his own. He was second secretary from 1804 until his retirement at the age of eighty one in 1845 with only a brief interruption during 1806 and 1807. Unlike most of his predecessors in this role, he remained in office regardless of the political affiliation of the government and served thirteen administrations. During this time he also wrote 195 geographical reviews, mostly about exploration, for the *Quarterly Review*; became a friend of its publisher, John Murray, who published many of Barrow's own books; received the degree of LL.D. from Edinburgh University for his promotion of science and his literary endeavours; was elected to the Royal Society and to the Linnaean Society of London; and was a founder member of the Royal Geographical Society. He was created a baronet in 1835. As a Fellow of the Royal Society he became a friend of its President, Sir Joseph Banks, with whom he shared a passion for exploration. Barrow's position at the Admiralty allowed him to fulfil their joint ambitions. He championed the sending of a succession of British expeditions to discover a sea route from the Atlantic to the Pacific, north of the Canadian mainland – the North West Passage. By

Figure 5.2. The house at Dragley Beck, Ulverston, where John Barrow was born *(photograph: Rob David)*

1844 much charting had been done, a number of possible routes had been established and only about 900 miles still awaited navigation. As a final act he submitted a 'Proposal for an attempt to complete the discovery of the North West Passage' to First Lord of the Admiralty, Lord Haddington. The consequence was the fitting out of a new expedition in 1845 under the leadership of Sir John Franklin. When Barrow died on 23 November 1848, concern about the fate of this expedition was growing and the first search expeditions had already been despatched.

Although Barrow, in the words of Fergus Fleming, 'had spent his life trying to escape' Ulverston, ironically it was on the edge of this small market town in Furness that his colossal memorial was to be constructed. The *Ulverston Advertiser* had described Sir John in a eulogy written at the time of his death as 'a great and estimable character [who] serves to inspire others with a laudable ambition to walk in his steps'. Barrow deserved, according to the paper, 'that best monument that could possibly be erected to the memory of a human being'. The resulting Hoad Monument, a 100-foot-high tower in the shape of Eddystone Lighthouse, was built with the proceeds of a public subscription (Figure 5.3).

Given that Barrow was in effect a retired civil servant, albeit with forty years of almost continuous service, it was a bold move to establish a committee to launch an appeal. His career had brought him into contact with eminent people in many walks of life. He had met administrators, diplomats and adventurers during his early travels in China, Africa and the Arctic, although many of them had pre-deceased him. At the Admiralty he had worked with

Figure 5.3. The Hoad Monument, Ulverston *(photograph: Rob David)*

most of the senior naval personnel of the first half of the nineteenth century. Although by temperament conservative, he had also met, or corresponded with, ministers in all of the governments since 1804. As the organiser of numerous journeys of exploration he knew many of the leading naval commanders and officers whom the Admiralty employed. As a fellow of the Royal Society, the Royal Geographical Society and the Linnaean Society of London, he was acquainted with many of the country's leading scientists, travellers and geographers. There could have been few other people with such a range of wealthy and influential friends, colleagues and acquaintances. All such people were potential subscribers to the memorial, as were, of course, family members and the citizens of his home town. His family, although fairly extensive and reasonably prosperous, had no land or inherited wealth. Sir John had been a self-made man, a point emphasised in the obituary that appeared in the *Ulverston Advertiser*, and it is perhaps this aspect of his career, as much as his work as a civil servant, that appealed in particular to the Ulverston subscribers (Figure 5.4).

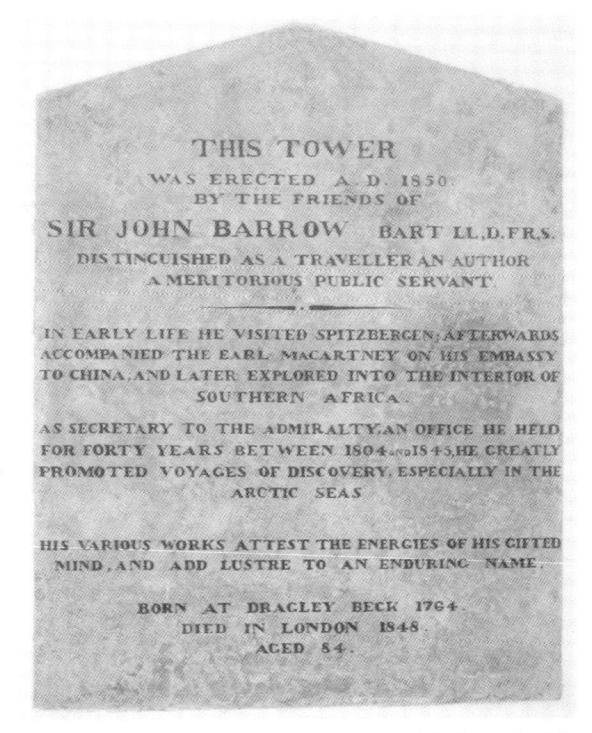

Figure 5.4. The Sir John Barrow memorial plaque inside the Hoad Monument *(photograph: Rob David)*

Apart from Adelaide, the Queen Dowager, and a few other women supporters, the overwhelming majority of subscribers to the appeal were men. Sir John's professional life had been spent entirely in a man's world, so this was not surprising, but they came from all walks of life. There were ten named members of the aristocracy including the Earls of Burlington and of Lonsdale from Cumbria. As he had been in post during so many governments it is not surprising to find that many senior politicians contributed to the appeal. These included prime ministers such as Viscount Palmerston and Robert Peel. Additionally nearly all the first lords of the Admiralty who had not pre-deceased him, subscribed. Some, such as Viscount Melville, had been supportive of Barrow's Arctic activities; others such as The Rt. Hon. Sir James Graham Bt. had family connections with Cumbria. Barrow's extraordinary range of naval contacts is shown in the professional roles of many of the subscribers. Hydrographer of the Navy, Admiral Sir Francis Beaufort, had been in post since 1829, and Sir Benjamin Outram, a surgeon and naval officer, had become an inspector of fleets and hospitals in 1841. Subscriptions were received from civil servants of every rank - from first secretaries such as the Rt. Hon. John Wilson Croker, who had recommended Barrow for a baronetcy, to the lowly Admiralty official Piers O'Barrington.

Contacting Barrow's explorers was not so easy. At the time of his death Barrow's African explorers had mostly pre-deceased him, and many of the Arctic explorers were in the north searching for Sir John Franklin and his second-in-command, Captain James Fitzjames, as well as their ships' companies all of whom had disappeared somewhere in the Canadian Arctic. Sir John Richardson and Dr. John Rae were in Canada travelling north to the shore of the Arctic Ocean; Sir James Clark Ross was following in Franklin's footsteps through Lancaster Sound and into the maze of islands and straits in that area; and Thomas Moore, who had been sent to the western Arctic via the Pacific to await Franklin's emergence from the North West Passage was beginning to search the coastline north of Russian America, now Alaska. Many other veterans of Barrow's Arctic expeditions such as Horatio Austin, Erasmus Ommanney, Sherard Osborn, William Penny, and Robert McClure were either in the Arctic or on their way there. The more elderly explorers such as Sir George Back, Sir William Edward Parry and Captain F. W. Beechey were contributing their expertise through the so-called 'Arctic Council', which was advising on the search for Franklin. Many of these men did subscribe, but *in absentia* through their wives or friends.

Sir John's immense range of interests is exemplified through the extraordinary range of other subscribers who were happy to support the appeal. The presidents of the Royal Society, the Linnaean Society and the Royal Geographical Society at or around the time of his death all contributed. Others included the engineers Isambard Kingdom Brunel and James Rendel; the publisher John Murray, son of the John Murray who had published many of Barrow's books, his numerous articles for the *Quarterly Review*, and the books written by the Arctic explorers on their return from the voyages that Barrow promoted; authors such as William O'Byrne, compiler of *Naval Biographical Dictionary*; the portraitist Stephen Pearce who was about to start work on one of his largest canvases, *The Arctic Council discussing a plan of search for Sir John Franklin*, which featured Sir John Barrow's son, and a portrait of Sir John on the wall; and James Ramsden who was becoming a key figure in the development of the Furness Railway and the port of Barrow. At the other end of the scale was Thomas Downs, a Portsmouth sailor who according to the letter enclosing his one pound subscription, had heard about the testimonial from a newspaper, and wanted to show his gratitude towards Sir John for finding an opening for him in the navy. The list of subscribers was completed by a small number of the citizens of Ulverston: a surgeon Bernard Gilpin, the vicar the Rev. Richard Gwillym, the postmaster Moses Mawson, and the proprietor of the *Ulverston Advertiser*, Stephen Soulby, as well as a group of family members.

The appeal raised over £1182 within about a year, and this enabled the organising committee to embark on a substantial memorial, but there was no consensus as to what form it should take. At that time statues were not considered to be the memorial of choice and an obelisk was seen as a memorial more suited to less successful appeals. Some London subscribers favoured a column, while the hydrographer of the navy, Admiral Sir Francis Beaufort, introduced the idea that a memorial could be useful as well as imposing, and suggested that it should be 'made subservient to some distinct and notable benefit to the navigation of anyone of the adjoining ports or channels'. A local correspondent in the *Ulverston Advertiser* disagreed with the idea of such a sea-mark, as given the location of the hills in the neighbourhood of Ulverston, 'the erection of a column of this kind would not be of the slightest use to mariners'. He proposed a 'memorial of a more useful character', which for him meant using the money to 'increase the endowment of Town Bank School, in which this worthy baronet was taught the rudiments of his education'. The idea that a monument should be useful was an unfamiliar concept. Consequently, the newspaper returned to the subject pointing out that, despite the previous objection, the construction of a column on a neighbouring eminence could also have wider economic benefits through 'inducing pleasure-seekers and curiosity-lovers to visit the town... [so] that its trade and commerce would be materially improved'. The paper went on to urge the town to support both the monument and the endowment of the school for the benefit of the community.

When the first list of subscribers was announced in *The Times* on 15th September 1849 it was clear that the idea of a sea-mark had found most favour, as the preamble contained the following statement from the organising committee:

> 'Sir John Barrow's whole life was passed in usefully serving his country, and his friends being desirous that this memorial should be also practically useful, have resolved that it should be so placed as to serve as a Sea-mark for the navigation of an intricate and dangerous part of Morecambe Bay, the site on the Hoad-hill, at Ulverston, having been approved by the Trinity House'.

This idea was approved by the Admiralty, and the *Ulverston Advertiser* urged that the monument could usefully take the form of 'an Observatory, Lighthouse, and a Signal and Telegraph Station'. Unsurprisingly, given the additional cost and negligible maritime benefit, these more ambitious suggestions were not followed up. By May 1850, Mr Andrew Trimen's design of a sea-mark in imitation of the Eddystone Lighthouse (but as a light was not to be included, it was never seen as being a lighthouse) had been chosen by the committee, and Trinity House had donated £100 to the appeal.

On the 15th May 1850 Ulverston 'presented an animated appearance' as the sun shone on the town. A procession made its way to the summit of Hoad Hill forming:

> 'one of the grandest and most imposing spectacles it has ever been our lot to witness...the serpentine walks became gradually filled, until from the top to the bottom, an apparently endless chain of living links of human machinery appeared to have been set in motion. The effect was heightened by the display of numerous gay colored (sic) flags, which imparted to the whole, the character of a grand romance rather than a scene of reality'(Figure 5.5).

Ulverston was clearly enjoying the ceremony of the laying of the foundation stone of the sea-mark. It was an occasion for the people of Ulverston and Furness to celebrate at someone else's expense. Many may have been unsure who Sir John was, as he had failed to visit his place of birth for fifty years, and fewer still may have read, let alone been persuaded by, his statement in his 1847 autobiography that he could not 'forego the opportunity now afforded me to say a word in favour of my native place, where my earliest, and I believe my happiest, days were passed', but this was an event unparalleled in the town's recent past, and Ulverstonians were determined to take advantage of this 'best monument that could possibly be erected to the memory of a human being'.

The inclusion of Hoad Hill and a vignette of Sir John Barrow's Monument on the new edition of the Admiralty's chart for Morecambe Bay published in 1850 demonstrated a belief in its value for navigation. The monument was completed in July 1851 after some repairs necessitated by a lightning strike. That its potential as an attraction for townspeople and visitors was being recognised is revealed by further discussion locally about the layout of paths and the planting of shrubs on the hill. The memorial was to be a memento to Sir John, an impressive and utilitarian structure of value both to seafarers and to travellers crossing Morecambe Bay, and additionally a place of recreation for townspeople and an attraction for visitors. These included the widowed Lady Jane Franklin and her niece Sophia Cracroft on their visit to the Lake District in the autumn of 1860. Few memorials of that period had so many demands placed on it.

Second Secretary Sir John Barrow enabled the further exploration of the Arctic during the first half of the nineteenth century. Amongst the explorers that Barrow was responsible for sending to the Arctic were William Edward Parry, John Ross, James Clark Ross and John Richardson. Their lives were connected with Cumbria in a variety of ways.

Figure 5.5. The *Illustrated London News* report of the laying of the foundation stone of the memorial to Sir John Barrow, 25 May 1850.

Sir John Richardson (1787-1865) and his retirement in Grasmere

Sir John Richardson was one of the explorers who took part in the nineteenth century naval expeditions in search of the North West Passage (Figure 5.6). He had a strong association with Cumbria, having retired there in 1855. He spent the last ten years of his life at Lancrigg in Grasmere, the property of Elizabeth Fletcher (1770-1858), whose daughter Mary (1802-1880) was Sir John's third wife – 'a marriage that seems to please everybody' as Harriet Martineau of Ambleside wrote in 1847 (Figure 5.7). Lancrigg, a 'beautiful little farm', had been bought by Elizabeth Fletcher in 1839 and enlarged on Wordsworth's advice. It was probably the Kendal architect George Webster (1797-1864) who used the increasingly fashionable vernacular when designing the extensions and remodelling the interior. The Richardsons therefore took possession of a recently modernised house. Helped, according to the 1861 census, by a housemaid, a waiting maid and a coachman, John and Mary made Lancrigg their home, albeit sharing the house with Elizabeth Fletcher until her death in 1858. It was a place to return to, and recover in, after their frequent journeys around Britain and overseas. In Sir John, the small community of Grasmere acquired a true polymath. As well as his skills as doctor and surgeon, he was knowledgeable about geology, mammalogy, ichthyology, botany, lichenology and ornithology.

John Richardson was born in Dumfries in 1787 and later trained as a doctor and natural historian. His medical and scientific expertise meant that he was ideally placed to join the 1819 Admiralty

Figure 5.6. Portrait of Sir John Richardson by Stephen Pearce, 1850. National Portrait Gallery 909 (© *National Portrait Gallery, London*)

Figure 5.7. Lancrigg, Grasmere. Sir John Richardson's home 1855-1865 *(photograph: Rob David)*

expedition to search for the North West Passage as surgeon and scientist. This expedition, commanded by John Franklin, travelled northwards through Canada during 1819 and 1820, descended the Coppermine River in canoes in 1821 and charted some 500 miles of the difficult, unexplored coastline of the 'Polar Sea'. The return journey across what explorers called the 'Barren Grounds' was one of the most difficult in the history of Arctic exploration. Storms, freezing temperatures, a shortage of food, a lack of cooperation by some of the Iroquois *voyageurs* who accompanied them, and the failure of the fur companies to leave supplies at designated locations, left Franklin's team weak and exhausted. They were reduced to eating lichens, warble-fly larvae and even their spare boots. Needing to cross the Coppermine River and having no boats, Richardson volunteered to swim the 180 yards to the other side. The cold water defeated him, and the others had to haul on the line and drag him back. When he was eventually able to crawl back into his tent, the others stripping him of his wet clothes saw the state of his body, a mirror of their own. 'I cannot describe' wrote Franklin 'what everyone felt at beholding the skeleton which the doctor's debilitating frame exhibited'.

Richardson's stamina, his skills as a doctor and his decisiveness in times of trouble did much to ensure their survival. The expedition returned to England in 1822. Franklin had led his men across some 5500 miles of northern Canada, but at the cost of eleven lives from his twenty-strong team. Despite having to abandon much of his equipment and specimens, Richardson had begun to transform scientific knowledge of the natural history of northern Canada, a task he continued during Franklin's second expedition of 1825-27. This time all went well. He travelled with Franklin to the mouth of the great Mackenzie River and explored and mapped 863 miles of unknown coastline towards the Coppermine River. On his return Richardson wrote three of the four volumes of *Fauna Boreali-Americana* and contributed most of the plants for Hooker's *Flora Boreali-Americana*, - two publications that set the standard for the scientific results of nineteenth-century expeditions.

In 1828 Richardson was appointed chief medical officer of Melville Naval Hospital, Chatham, in 1838 senior physician at the Royal Naval Hospital Haslar, Gosport, and in 1840 he became an inspector of hospitals. While at Haslar he made the hospital into one of the world's pre-eminent research establishments into natural history and comparative anatomy. Richardson concentrated on the study of ichthyology and became a world expert. In 1848 he left for the Canadian Arctic again, this time with Dr. John Rae, in order to search for his old friend Sir John Franklin from whom nothing had been heard since he sailed into Lancaster Sound in search of the North West Passage in 1845. Richardson returned to England to resume his medical career in 1849, acknowledging that he was by then too old for Arctic exploration and leaving Rae to continue the search for Franklin. However, he continued to support Lady Jane Franklin in her efforts to convince others to continue the search for Sir John and his companions, and in 1855 wrote to *The Times* to champion Franklin's claim to have discovered the North West Passage six months earlier than Captain McClure who, while searching for Franklin, had passed through a passage (albeit travelling in part on sea ice rather than by navigating a ship) from west to east during his expedition between 1850 and 1854.

In 1855 Sir John applied for the post of director general of the medical department of the Royal Navy, but at sixty-seven he was considered too old. He continued to collect honours, however. To his fellowship of the Royal Society, his knighthood and his appointment as a companion of the Bath, he added the Royal Society's 'royal Medal' in 1856 and an honorary doctorate from University College, Dublin in 1857. During his retirement in Grasmere he was as active as ever. As a member of the Admiralty's 'Arctic Council', of numerous parliamentary committees concerned with Arctic matters, and of many other societies, he attended meetings across the British Isles. He visited friends and travelled extensively in France and Italy. He corresponded with, and visited, Florence Nightingale, and in matters of mutual interest such as improving hospital conditions in the Navy, he 'was glad to find that our opinions were precisely alike'. It was said of him that 'he was constantly engaged in literary labours and would walk miles to prescribe for the poorest person in the valley of Grasmere who might require his aid'. During the winter of 1856-7 he wrote a number of entries for the *Encyclopaedia Britannica*, including one on 'Ichthyology' and another about Sir John Franklin. The latter entry became the nineteenth century's most repeated version of the Franklin story. Charles Dickens found 'Richardson's manly friendship, and love of Franklin, one of the noblest things I ever knew in my life. It makes one's heart beat high, with a sort of sacred joy'. Richardson's phrase 'They Forged the Last Link with their Lives' was repeated on the nation's memorial statue to Franklin and his men, unveiled in London in 1866, a year after Richardson's death. In 1861, by expanding on his contributions for the *Encyclopaedia Britannica*, he completed his history of exploration, *The Polar Regions*.

Richardson was also a keen gardener and fell walker. On 6 November, 1863, the day after his seventy-sixth birthday, he 'took a holiday and went

Figure 5.8. The memorial to Sir John Richardson in St Oswald's Church, Grasmere *(photograph: Rob David)*

to the top of Helm Crag, and had a survey of the valley from "the Lion and the Lamb"'. He died peacefully in bed on 5 June 1865, after a day spent visiting friends in Rydal and Ambleside. Typically he had taken the Anglo-Saxon version of King Alfred's *History of the World by Orosius* to bed with him. His death was 'much lamented in Grasmere where he had helped the poor in sickness and sorrow'. He was buried in St Oswald's Church in Grasmere where the memorial plaque inside the church highlights his role as 'the constant companion of Sir John Franklin in Arctic exploration' (Figure 5.8). His biographer David Stewart wrote: 'his life was perhaps a life of industry more than a life of a genius, but it was a full, good life, and in many ways a great life. It is not every day that we meet in one person – surgeon, physician, sailor, soldier, administrator, explorer, naturalist, author, and scholar, who has been eminent in some roles and commendable in all'.

While Richardson was working at Haslar his friend and senior officer was Sir William Edward Parry, another of Barrow's Arctic explorers, who had been at the forefront in the search for the North West Passage. Parry too has unusual and interesting connections with Cumbria.

Sir William Edward Parry (1790-1855), the mural at Crosthwaite and the inscription at Ecclerigg

In 1852 Sir William Edward Parry retired as captain-superintendent of Haslar Royal Naval Hospital and came to Keswick for a holiday 'where he derived much enjoyment from his first acquaintance with the beautiful scenery of the English lakes'. So far as is known this was his only visit to Cumbria. However, his fame as a polar explorer had been such that, several decades earlier, his portrait had been painted on a bulkhead overlooking the staircase at Tower Hill, Crosthwaite (Figure 5.9), and his name was carved on a quarry face at Ecclerigg on Lake Windermere (Figure 5.12).

The painting was discovered under layers of wallpaper and paint at Tower Hill in 1954. It had been painted onto three vertical wooden panels which form both a staircase wall and the back of a built-in bedroom cupboard. At the time of Parry's Arctic voyages (1818-1827) Tower Hill was occupied by Richard Cartmell, a farmer, whose obituary, which was printed in both *The Westmorland Advertiser and Kendal Chronicle* and in the *Westmorland Gazette* on April 2, 1831, reads:

> On the 20 ult. at Crosthwaite Green near Kendal of a protracted illness. Mr Richard Cartmell aged 59. He was a very ingenious man, whose talents have been confined to his own immediate neighbourhood. As an artist he excelled, being self-taught, and has left behind him a number of portraits sketched from memory after having seen the person, amongst whom are Lord and Col. Lowther, Lord Brougham, the late Sir Daniel le Fleming and the Rev. J. Strickland, with many others in general good likeness.

It seems likely that Richard Cartmell was the artist of Parry's portrait. The naive quality of the portrait points to the artist being 'self-taught', and originally there were at least two other similarly naïve murals in the house, one of a young boy and another of an angel-like figure.

How did Richard Cartmell know what Parry looked like? As there is no reason why Cartmell should have met Parry between 1818, when Parry's first voyage to the Arctic was extensively reported, and 1831

Figure 5.9. The painting of Captain William Edward Parry at Tower Hill, Crosthwaite *(reproduced by courtesy of John Holmes. Photograph: Rob David)*

when Cartmell died, it seems likely that Cartmell based his painting on a picture of Parry. The Crosthwaite portrait is clearly based on that by Samuel Drummond, a largely self-taught London artist, who painted the most commonly reproduced portrait of Parry in 1820 (Figure 5.10). Drummond was a prolific portraitist who was able to 'produce a portrait in a single sitting lasting an hour and a half, and charged eight guineas for a three quarter length'. His ability to work at speed would have been helpful to a busy man like Parry. There are two versions of this painting, one of which was on display for a few weeks at the Royal Academy in London but it is unlikely that Cartmell would travel to the capital for such a show. The other was originally owned by John Barrow (1808-98), the son of Sir John Barrow. Despite the family's Cumbrian connections there is no reason to think that it ever hung in Cumbria, so how could Cartmell have seen it?

It is more likely that Cartmell saw one of the engravings based on Drummond's picture. Several engravings were made and published in the years after 1820, but the one most likely to have been the prototype for the Crosthwaite painting was created by J. Thomson

Figure 5.10. Portrait of Captain William Edward Parry painted by Samuel Drummond, 1820. National Portrait Gallery 5053 *(© National Portrait Gallery, London)*

Figure 5.11. Engraving of Captain William Edward Parry, by J. Thomson, 1 March, 1821, for the *European Magazine and London Review*.

and published in the *European Magazine and London Review* (Figure 5.11). This engraving is a reasonably faithful reproduction of Drummond's portrait except that Parry's lower left arm and left hand were omitted, as in the Crosthwaite picture. Most significantly Thomson incorporated a title beneath the portrait which, except for the inclusion of dates in the last line, is identical to that in the Crosthwaite painting:

Captn. W.E. Parry R.N.
Commander of the Polar Expedition
(1819-20)

The engraving was published in the February 1821 edition of the *European Magazine and London Review*, a monthly journal that had a wide circulation, which Cartmell must have either subscribed to or seen in a local reading room or in the house of an acquaintance. The fact that Cartmell 'sketched from memory' may explain the reversal of the figure and some of the other differences between the engraving and his portrait.

It was probably Parry's fame that prompted Cartmell to paint his portrait on the wall of Tower Hill. Parry had been second-in-command to John Ross during the voyages in search of the North West Passage in 1818. Parry was convinced that the Croker Mountains which Ross claimed had prevented them from exploring Lancaster Sound did not exist, and he had written to his family on his return 'I know it [the North West Passage] is in existence, and not very hard to find'. Lieutenant Parry was chosen by Barrow to command the next expedition charged with discovering the North West Passage in 1819.

The return from his second voyage in 1820 ensured Parry's fame. Parry had sailed with two ships, *Hecla* (in which he sailed) and *Griper* in May 1819, passing through Lancaster Sound without seeing Ross's Croker Mountains and reaching Melville Island where the two ships spent the winter. Heavy pack ice during 1820 frustrated his plans, Parry was unable to sail further west, and the ships returned to London in November 1820. Despite not finding the North West Passage, Parry had been extremely successful. His ships had travelled over half the distance between Greenland and the Bering Strait and had proved, for the first time, that it was possible to winter in the Arctic. In addition the expedition came back with much valuable geographical and scientific material. On his return Parry was promoted to the rank of commander. He received the freedom of Bath, his native city; was elected to the Royal Society; and, along with the ship's company, received the parliamentary grant of £5000 which had been offered as a reward for those who should first pass the meridian of 110°W within the Arctic Circle. Both Ross's and Parry's 1818 voyage and Parry's 1819-20 expedition were widely reported and best-selling narratives published. Cartmell could have read one of these in the *European Magazine and London Review's* January 1821 issue. Thomson's engraving in the following number was accompanied by a eulogy in praise of 'our deserving countryman, Captain Parry, who has on two successive occasions distinguished himself by the display of talents and energies, which have excited the admiration of the country'. Taken together the account, the engraving and the eulogy could have prompted Cartmell to paint a picture of a national hero.

Parry's only other expedition to achieve national fame was his fifth and final Arctic voyage to Spitsbergen in 1827. From there he hoped to reach the North Pole, but his attempt was frustrated because the ice floes on which he was sledging drifted south almost as fast as he attempted to travel north. His crew was therefore expending considerable energy but making very little headway. Despite this he achieved the furthest north (82°40'23"N) yet reached, a record that stood until 1876, when it was overtaken by sledging parties from Sir George Nares's expedition. Parry's achievement was celebrated widely in Britain and Europe. The publicity surrounding him in 1828 and 1829 might have prompted Cartmell to paint the picture, using the old engraving dating back to 1821, but on balance the Crosthwaite painting was probably painted during, or soon after, 1821.

Parry's name also appears carved onto a slate slab at Ecclerigg Quarry, Windermere, along with that of Ross, accompanied by the date 1835, but it is far from clear why Parry's name was inscribed (Figure 5.12). In 1829 he had left Britain to take up employment as commissioner of the Australian Agricultural Company. Although he was successful in that role, his work was of no significance back in Britain. By 1835 he had returned to Britain, and when his name on the rock face was inscribed, possibly by William Longmire of Troutbeck, he was assistant poor-law commissioner for Norfolk, well out of the public eye. It may have been the case that Parry's earlier fame as a polar explorer survived his eight years of subsequent obscurity, or it may have been his association with John and James Clark Ross that triggered the association in the mind of the carver. Parry had been second-in-command to John Ross in 1818, and had been accompanied by Ross's nephew, James Clark Ross, on all his subsequent Arctic expeditions. Whatever the reasons, at that time John Ross and Parry were probably the two Arctic explorers whose exploits were most well known to the public.

Sir John Ross (1777-1856) and Sir James Clark Ross (1800-1862) and the Inscription at Ecclerigg

On the same slate slab at Ecclerigg, the name 'Ross' was carved at the top of one of the two lists of names (Figure 5.13). In 1835 Captain John Ross and his nephew, Commander James Clark Ross, were also famous polar explorers, but neither had a connection to Cumbria (Figures 5.14 and 5.15).

Figure 5.12. The name 'Parry' carved on the rock slab at Ecclerigg Quarry, Windermere *(Photograph: Maggie Sale)*

Figure 5.13. The name 'Ross' carved on the rock slab at Ecclerigg Quarry, Windermere *(Photograph: Maggie Sale)*

Therefore, as with the case of Cartmell's portrait of Parry, their fame must almost certainly have inspired the mason, but by carving the name 'Ross' on the slab he may have been referring to either or both men. The two Ross's had returned from an expedition to the North-West Passage in 1833 as if from the dead. As Sir John had fallen out-of-favour with Barrow after the less-than-successful expedition in 1818, Ross persuaded the distiller Felix Booth to provide financial support for a voyage to Lancaster Sound and the unexplored straits beyond. *Victory* departed in 1829 but the vessel was beset and had eventually to be abandoned. This resulted in the expedition spending four winters in the Arctic. By 1833 it was assumed in Britain that the entire crew had perished, so their rescue by the whale ship *Isabella* and their return in October 1833 received extensive coverage in the national and regional press and was the cause of national rejoicing. The *Westmorland Gazette*, for example, printed the developing story in almost every weekly edition between 19 October and the end of November. It became apparent that this voyage had resulted in the most significant achievements. The Gulf of Boothia had been discovered and hundreds of miles of previously unknown coast had been surveyed. Their map of Boothia was the best available for over a century, and the expedition's continuous series of scientific observations were not bettered until modern times. They returned with large natural history collections, and more information about the landscapes and 'Eskimos' than any previous expedition. But perhaps the highlight was James Clark Ross's discovery of the North Magnetic Pole.

The scientific achievements were already being broadcast by December

Figure 5.14. Portrait of Captain John Ross by James Green, 1833. National Portrait Gallery 314 *(© National Portrait Gallery, London)*

Figure 5.15. Captain James Clark Ross by R. M. Hodgetts, after John Robert Wildman, mezzotint, published 1835. National Portrait Gallery D4105 *(© National Portrait Gallery, London)*

1833 when James Clark Ross read a paper 'On the Position of the North Magnetic Pole' to the Royal Society. Interest in the expedition was maintained when early in 1834 a panorama opened at Leicester Square in London. *A View of the Continent of Boothia, discovered by Captain Ross* was painted by the proprietor, Robert Burford, from sketches by John Ross. A few weeks later a 'Grand Scenic Representation of Captain Ross's Expedition to the North Pole' opened at Royal Gardens, Vauxhall. This involved an enormous panoramic painting covering over 60,000 square feet of canvas, the last part of which included 'Immense Icebergs, upwards of seventy feet high' and included at the close of the show, 'a gigantic image of Captain Ross in Polar Costume, rising from amidst the Icebergs', as well as 'A Superb Exhibition of Fire Works'. The reviewer for *The Times* was overwhelmed by the spectacle: 'It is almost impossible by verbal description to convey an accurate idea of the effect of this exhibition, which is in every respect the most interesting both in general arrangement and detailed execution that has been submitted to the visitors to these gardens'.

In December John Ross was given a knighthood, and in early 1835 he was in south-west Scotland seeking election as a tory for the Wigtown Burghs, the area of Galloway in which he had been born. This provided additional publicity although he was not well received in this traditional Whig area, and on the 14 January 1835, the *Dumfries Times* reported that 'Sir John Ross has abandoned his canvass of the burghs. All the cold he felt at the pole was nothing to the coldness of his reception by the electors'. In April, John Ross's account of the expedition was published in two volumes. Newspapers such as *The Times* and *The Observer* were generally enthusiastic, although his old antagonist, Sir John Barrow, who had blamed Ross for the failure of the 1818 expedition to find the North West Passage, berated the book in *The Quarterly Review*. For eighteen months after their return in the autumn of 1833 the Ross's, especially John Ross, had been in the glare of publicity. Despite failure in the Wigtown Burghs and criticism from Sir John Barrow, their achievements had been lionised across the nation. No other polar explorers, or for that matter any explorer, were more likely to have caught the eye of the Ecclerigg carver, when he chose to inscribe the name 'Ross' on the rock face in 1835. Despite the appointment of James Clark Ross in December 1835 to lead the Admiralty's rescue expedition to search for the whaling vessels that Captain Brass of *Alfred* (see Chapter 4) had reported as trapped in the ice in Davis Strait, an event that probably came too late to influence the carvings on the Ecclerigg slabs, it was probably John Ross whom the carver had in mind. The Ecclerigg carvings, coming so soon after the Crosthwaite painting, confirm the impact polar exploration had on the popular imagination in a relatively remote area of the country such as Cumbria.

[A discussion about the significance of the eclectic list of names on the Ecclerigg carvings can be found in B. Tyson, 'William Edward Parry (1790-1855) Explorer – a response' and R.

David, 'William Edward Parry (1790-1855) Explorer – reply to a response', *Transactions of the Cumberland and Westmorland Antiquarian and Archaeological Society*, Third Series, Vol. X, 2010, 253-259.]

OTHER CUMBRIANS IN THE NORTH WEST PASSAGE

Some members of ships' companies on private expeditions in search of the North West Passage included sailors born in, or connected to, Cumbria. One of the most famous of these expeditions was the previously-mentioned voyage of Captain John Ross in *Victory* in 1829. On this voyage George Taylor was the third mate. He had been born in Lancaster but had served his apprenticeship of five years as a ship's carpenter in Ulverston in the building yard of James Hart. Taylor then served in a number of merchant vessels, and was master of *Victory* when she was purchased by Ross. Ross was so impressed with him that he was invited to stay on as third mate. *Victory* spent the winter of 1829-30 near Boothia Peninsula. Unfortunately 'in [April] 1830, while on a [sledge] journey [across the Boothia Isthmus] with Commander [James Clark] Ross, he [Taylor] got his right foot frostbitten; and being in the first instance neglected, ended in the amputation of his foot, two inches above the toes'. This left him unable to walk, which given what was about to happen, was a near-disaster. During the summers of 1830 and 1831 Ross was unable to extricate his ship from the ice and he and the ship's company were forced to winter in the same area in 1830-31 and 1831-32. During the winter months in early 1832 Ross abandoned *Victory* and pulled the ship's boats across the ice in order to retreat to Baffin Bay. Taylor, unable to walk, had to be carried on a makeshift sledge. However, heavy pack ice during the summer prevented their escape and they were forced to spend a fourth winter, this time at an old camping site which had been used by Sir William Edward Parry. Finally in August 1833 they were able to use their boats to reach Lancaster Sound where they were picked up by the astonished crew of the whaler *Isabella*. Later Ross wrote that when he had identified himself to the mate 'he assured me that I had been dead two years'. He described their condition, which no doubt reflected the state of George Taylor too, on boarding the whaler:

> Unshaven since I know not when, dirty, dressed in the rags of wild beasts…and starved to the very bones, our gaunt and grim looks…made us feel …what we really were, as well as what we seemed to others. All, everything was to be done at once; it was washing, dressing, shaving, eating, all intermingled…while in the midst of it all there were interminable questions to be asked and answered on all sides.

Isabella had not completed her season's 'fishing', so Ross and his ship's company had to endure a further few weeks in Baffin Bay. When *Isabella* finally landed at Hull on 18 October, news of their miraculous survival had preceded them and they were given a civic welcome. Once this was over George Taylor rejoined his wife and family in Liverpool.

Although no Cumbrians sailed with Sir John Franklin in *Erebus* or *Terror*, both of which disappeared in the Arctic after 1845, some of the sailors who joined in the rescue attempts were from the county. William Foster of Whitehaven sailed with Sir James Clark Ross in *Enterprise* in 1848-49; Charles Campbell, a cooper from Carlisle, sailed in *Assistance* with Erasmus Ommaney in 1850-51; and Joseph Graham of Kelton in Westmorland sailed in *Assistance* with Sir Edward Belcher on a voyage which lasted from April 1852 to September 1854. All three sailed through Baffin Bay into Lancaster Sound, and wintered amongst the maze of partly explored channels and islands to the north of Canada. However, none of them returned with any conclusive evidence of the fate of Franklin and his crews. This was not the case for William Jones who lived in Ulverston between 1860 and 1862. He was employed as a dog-handler on Captain Francis Leopold McClintock's expedition in *Fox* in 1857-59. McClintock used dogs to supplement the more usual man-hauling of sledges, and Jones who had possibly learnt his dog-

Figure 5.16: Engraving 'McClintock's travelling party discovering remains of cairn at Cape Herschel', in F.L McClintock, *The Voyage of the 'Fox' in the Arctic Seas: A Narrative of the Discovery of the Fate of Sir John Franklin and his Companions*, London, John Murray, 1859.

handling skills as an employee of the Hudson's Bay Company, was responsible for those dogs alongside two Greenlanders. During the winter of 1858-9 it appears that he was one of the four expedition members who discovered the cairn at Point Victory on King William Island which contained the message that provided conclusive proof of what had happened to the expedition. Figure 5.16, a contemporary engraving that illustrated McClintock's narrative, depicts the discovery of another empty cairn but the scene would have been similar to that which took place at Point Victory. As dog-handler William Jones may well have been steering a sledge in the way the illustration shows. While sledging he discovered a flint and steel for striking a light, a relic of Franklin's expedition, which was later given to the Royal Naval Museum at Greenwich. After the expedition returned from the Arctic in the autumn of 1859, William Jones married and came to live in Ulverston. In 1861 he was recorded in the census living in Hart Street with his London-born wife Mary and their infant son who was appropriately named John Franklin Jones. He was employed as an iron merchant's clerk, but between 1860 and 1862 he also held the honorary post of 'Keeper of the Monument', which meant that he was responsible for the Hoad Monument and opening it for visitors (Figure 5.17). He would have been there when Lady Jane Franklin and her niece Sophia Cracroft visited the monument in October 1860. The family seem to have returned to London in 1862.

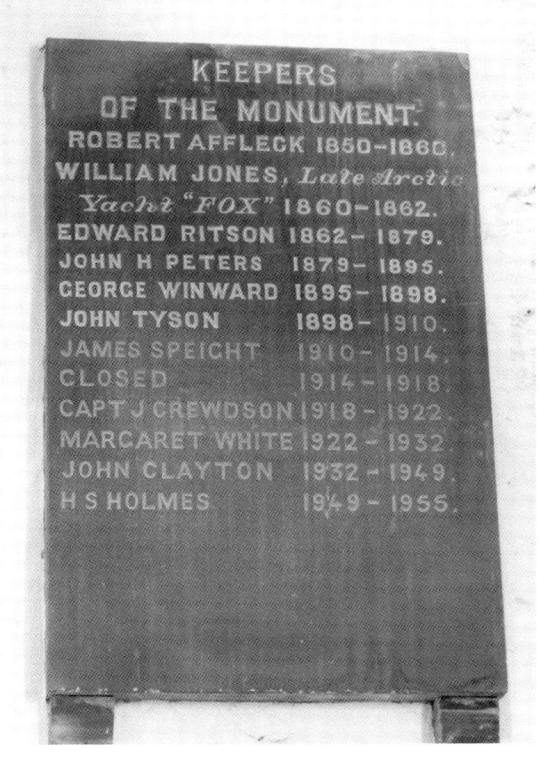

Figure 5.17: The plaque inside the Hoad Monument listing the 'Keepers of the Monument' including 'William Jones, late Arctic Yacht "Fox" 1860-1862' *(Photograph: Tess Pike)*

★ ★ ★ ★ ★

Suggested Further Reading

R. David, 'Building "That Best Monument": Memorialising Sir John Barrow at Ulverston', *Transactions of the Cumberland and Westmorland Antiquarian and Archaeological Society*, Third Series, Vol. VIII, 2008, 189-206.

R. David, 'The Painting of the Arctic Explorer Captain William Edward Parry (1790-1855) at Crosthwaite, near Kendal', *Transactions of the Cumberland and Westmorland Antiquarian and Archaeological Society*, Third Series, Vol. IX, 2009 175-185.

F. Fleming, *Barrow's Boys*, (London, Granta, 1998).

J. Layfield, *The Sir John Barrow Monument: The Story of Hoad 1848-1859*, (Ulverston, privately published, 2005).

C. Lloyd, *Mr Barrow of the Admiralty*, (London, Collins, 1970).

J. McIlraith, *Life of Sir John Richardson*, (London, Longmans, Green, 1868).

A. Parry, *Parry of the Arctic*, (London, Chatto and Windus, 1963).

M.J. Ross, *Polar Pioneers: John Ross and James Clark Ross*, (Montreal, McGill-Queen's University Press, 1994).

A. Savours, *The Search for the North West Passage*, (London, Chatham, 1999).

Chapter 6
'I am told I am going to an Unhabited land': The Yellow Earl in the Arctic, 1888-89

On 22 February 1888 the fifth Earl of Lonsdale – universally known as the Yellow Earl because of his predilection for the colour yellow in his coat-of-arms – sat in his cabin on board *The Republic* and wrote in his diary:

> I am told I am going to an Unhabited land. I cannot say I feel happy! As when I consider why I am going & without any of those dear to me, it would be false to pretend that I could be happy. It's no use crying over spilt milk. I am on the seas now & God knows what may be the result of my journey. Sport I hope. Happiness on my return I pray'.

Well might he have had some doubts about this journey, travelling as he was on the first leg of a journey that was to take him deep into the Arctic regions of Canada at the height of a northern winter (Figure 6.1).

Enthusiasm for Arctic exploration had waned in the 1860s as a result of two factors: firstly the retirement of Sir John Barrow in 1845, and secondly the return of Captain Francis Leopold McClintock in 1859 in *Fox*, with the conclusive evidence of the fate of Sir John Franklin and the entire ships' companies of HMS *Erebus* and HMS *Terror* some eleven years earlier. The *Hull Advertiser* voiced the thoughts of many when the paper expressed the hope that 'our countrymen will all agree that the mania of Arctic Expeditions has lasted long enough'. With the exception of Sir George Nares's North Pole expedition in 1875-76 which established a new furthest north at the cost of more deaths, this time to scurvy, British interest in Arctic exploration

Figure 6.1. The Earl of Lonsdale in clothing he brought back from the Arctic. This photograph was taken in the San Francisco studio of I.W. Taber in April 1889 on his way back to England *(Ownership lies with the Lowther Estate Trust)*

was limited to a few small expeditions to Spitsbergen and the Arctic regions north of Russia. Apart from some books on polar exploration on the library shelves at Lowther Castle in Cumbria, there is nothing to suggest that the fifth Earl of Lonsdale had any particular interest in the Arctic. It was therefore with some surprise that the English public learnt in mid-1888 from a report in the *Yorkshire Post*, that 'the Earl of Lonsdale is striking out a new path in Arctic exploration. He was met two months ago walking to the North Pole. Accompanied by 2 Eskimo guides he was pegging along in great spirits. Lord Lonsdale, who is known amongst the natives as "the man who walks fast" spoke confidently of being able to reach the North Pole'. The newspaper did not offer any explanation, beyond the claim that the North Pole was the objective, as to why Lord Lonsdale was there. The paper did, however, offer the wry observation that 'his new adventure is at any rate a better way of spending time than the weariness of lounging about the green rooms of London theatres'.

Hugh Lowther, the younger son of Henry, the third Earl of Lonsdale, had been born in 1857. With the deaths of his father in 1876, and his elder brother, St. George (the fourth Earl), in 1882, Hugh inherited the title and the estates and became the fifth Earl of Lonsdale (Figure 6.2). He had been brought up in the privileged environment of the very wealthy, and had been educated by private tutors in addition to his two years at Eton. As a young man his life revolved around London society and sport where his interests spanned fox-hunting, steeplechasing, horse racing, yachting, coursing

Figure 6.2. Lowther Castle in 1910 showing the Earl's fleet of yellow cars *(courtesy of Cumbria County Council, Carlisle Library)*

and boxing. He had married Lady Grace Cicelie Gordon in 1878. Little about his early life, beyond the Victorian aristocratic belief in self-worth, his enthusiasm for shooting, and an enjoyment of physical challenge, could have prepared him for his arrival in central Canada in the depths of winter in March 1888. Apart from his public claim that he was striking out for the North Pole, and his private hope that he would enjoy some sport, why was he there?

At the time, and subsequently, the Yellow Earl gave as many reasons for this journey as there were interviews to be given. Speaking to *The New York Times* on his arrival in the United States *en route* to Canada, he claimed that 'he was on the way to the North Pole....his one great desire had been to hunt the white bear of the frozen north....when he learned recently that a Scottish naturalist society wanted a bold adventurous man to go on a scientific expedition to the North Pole he decided to offer his services'. The three aims cited here represented a range of ambitions. The all-or-nothing aim of reaching the North Pole was clearly the most headline-grabbing, but also the most unrealistic given Nares's recent failure with all the resources of the Navy behind him, and Lonsdale's lack of expedition experience. It was probably sensible for him to temper that aim with the rather more achievable idea of hunting. For the committed hunter, African game had by now become all too familiar, and the Arctic was about to become the hunting environment of choice, as hunting trophies rarely contained the heads of polar bears and musk oxen. By hunting these animals the Earl positioned himself at the forefront of a new breed of wealthy traveller, seeking out ever more exotic destinations as travel became slightly easier. The claim that he had been asked to undertake scientific investigations by an ill-defined 'Scottish naturalist society', although repeated in various formulations throughout the Earl's life, was, given his idiosyncratic and minimal education, so unlikely that few could have been taken in by it. However, the idea that he had been commissioned to undertake scientific work suggests that he was seeking to place himself in the tradition of the explorer-scientist of the earlier nineteenth century, and thus provide a more acceptable basis for his journey.

By the time Lonsdale reached Winnipeg and was in communication with the Alaska Commercial Company through whose area of operation he was to pass, he had perhaps sensibly chosen to limit the aim of the journey to sport. In a letter to Lonsdale, the president of the company hoped that he would 'enjoy' his visit, and provided him with a letter of introduction to his agents in Alaska (which had been purchased from Russia by the United States in 1867) and along the Yukon River. This letter began unequivocally with the statement that 'the bearer of this letter, The Earl of Lonsdale, intends making a tour of Alaska and the Yukon River during the coming season, bent on pleasure and sport'.

However, a chance meeting with a new audience enabled the Earl to create yet another reason for the journey. He found himself accompanying Bishop William Bompas of the Church Missionary Society in the steamship *Wrigley* as they travelled north together along the Mackenzie River in northern Canada. The bishop reported later that Lonsdale had told him that his reason for travelling there was, at least in part, 'on account of the interest expressed by Her Majesty the Queen in the North and that Lord Lonsdale states that he is commanded to report to the Queen herself the conditions and needs of the Indians'. This was certainly a story that reflected Lonsdale's imperialistic and paternalistic approach and might impress a bishop, but although Queen Victoria was almost certainly involved in Lonsdale's adventure, it was for a rather different reason than stated.

It was not until after the Earl's death in 1944 and the publication by Douglas Sutherland of a new biography in 1965, that the probable underlying reason for Lonsdale being in the Canadian Arctic, rather than 'the green rooms of London theatres', was revealed. Sutherland saw Lonsdale's sudden disappearance in February 1888 as the consequence of the publicity that surrounded his affair with the actress Violet Cameron and his relationship with her husband David de Bensaude – an affair which kept the English and American public agog throughout the winter of 1887-8 (Figure 6.3). Newspapers on both sides of the ocean had a field day reporting the trans-Atlantic chases, the law suits and the court cases, of this *ménage à trois*. It seems that the Queen, perhaps fearful of Lonsdale's influence over the Prince of Wales, made it clear that she expected him to leave the country until the scandal had died down. This is the explanation accepted by Shepherd Krech in his academic treatise on Lord Lonsdale's journey, written to accompany an exhibition at the British Museum in 1989. His choice of the Canadian Arctic for his place of exile was no doubt influenced by the Britsh connection as well as by the support given to him by Sir John Rose, the head of the Hudson's Bay Company, and James Gordon Bennett who ran *The New York Times* and contributed to his expenses.

Figure 6.3. Photograph of Violet Cameron (1855-1910) probably taken during the 1880s *(©Theatre Museum, Victoria and Albert Museum, London)*

The details of his journey can, to an extent, be reconstructed from his journal and from letters written to his wife. He left Liverpool, accompanied only by his valet, Porter, on 22 February 1888 for New York where he disembarked on 3 March. On 6 March he travelled on to Montreal where he arrived the following day. He was very struck by the silence of the city since all carriages were on runners as everything was covered in snow. He met the leaders of the Canadian Pacific Railway Company and the Hudson's Bay Company, who promised their companies' help. He left by rail for Winnipeg on 8 March (Figure 6.4). Delayed by heavy snowfalls the train did not arrive there until 15 March. He took the opportunity to make some final purchases before travelling on to the small halt of Fort Qu'Appelle which he reached on 21 March. He arrived there during one of the coldest winters on record. The weather, snow and late break-up of the ice on the rivers and lakes were to cause him long delays. Accompanied by Porter, Billy McEwan, an employee of the Hudson's Bay Company, and a varying number of local guides, he left Fort Qu'Appelle and despite indifferent weather made fairly rapid progress northwards towards Fort McMurray by using a combination of horse-drawn vehicles and dog sledges,. By early April Porter, the valet, was struggling with the low temperatures, so Lonsdale sent him back home. The journal entry for 4 April described the conditions: 'Weather bitterly cold. We started on our journey, my first experience with dogs. Before we had gone a couple of

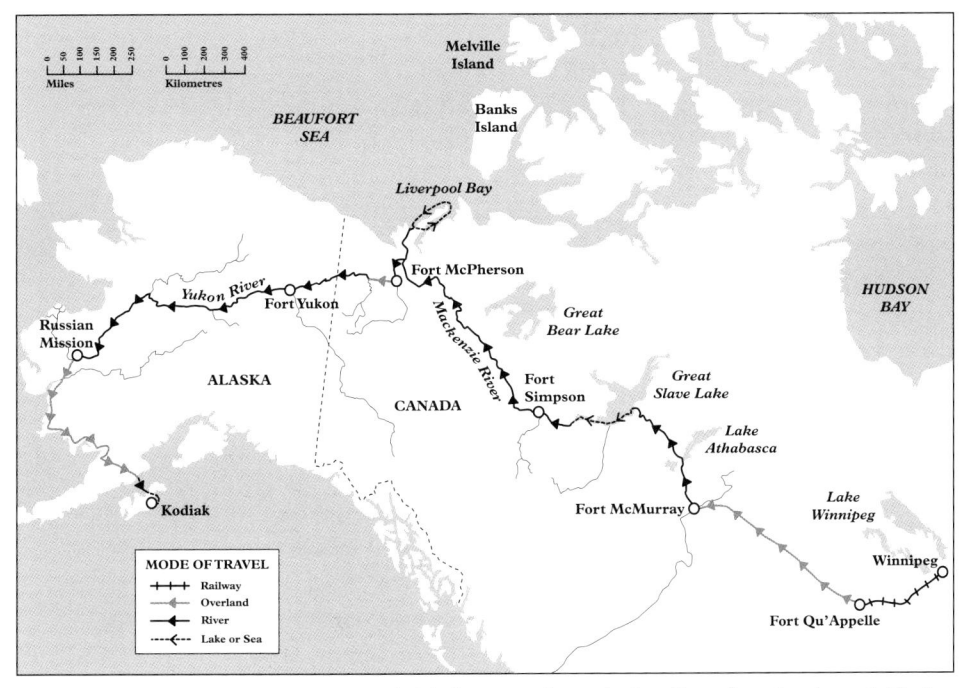

Figure 6.4. Map of the Earl of Lonsdale's journey through the Canadian Arctic and Alaska, 1888-89.

miles snow fell fast & heavy & a terrible snow storm impeded our journey'. Once at Fort McMurray, he then suffered delays and frustration during the spring break-up of the ice on the Athabasca and Clearwater Rivers. While he was trapped at Fort McMurray he took the opportunity to go hunting. He shot some grouse, geese and hawks, but failed to stalk moose or caribou successfully. He commented that it seemed a pity to kill beaver 'which will become extinct like the buffalo'.

Unaccustomed as he was to wearing snow shoes, and apparently wearing an inappropriate pair, he wrote after a day of moose stalking: 'We stalked for two hours. Up to this time I had strained my toe, nicked my ankle, twisted my foot and fallen 20 times from trying to walk on little snow shoes'. On 24 April he wrote to his wife: 'My dearest Bod [Lady Lonsdale]. I got a beautiful little duck which I skinned for you for a hat, a lovely silver breast and bronze back'. On 4 May he 'was awakened by the noise of distant thunder & the trembling of the house...and saw that the Athabaska had risen about 20 feet & ice blocks some tons weight pouring down the river at the rate of 10 miles an hour'. On 9 May he was able to cast off in a boat for Fort Chipewyan where he arrived on 15 May.

He found Fort Chipewyan with its population of native people, traders and company men 'pretty'. However, he was not encouraged by conversations with local guides who told him that 'there is nothing like the game in the country there was 10 or even 5 years ago. At one time 1000 moose and 2 to 3 thousand reindeer were brought to the station every six months- now 6 moose and 50 reindeer'. Rather despondently he wrote to Lady Lonsdale: 'from all I hear there is no sport to be had at all among big game of any sort. Very disappointed having come all this way – but live in hopes'. The decline in the quantity of game was caused by a combination of ecological change and population cycles as well as over-hunting and -trapping due in part to earlier Hudson's Bay Company activity, which since 1870 had been compounded by the government's abolition of the company's monopoly in the region. This had opened the area to unregulated and unsustainable exploitation by free hunters and native peoples and by others attracted there by the easier access provided by new steamboats on the rivers.

On 23 May 1888 he left Fort Chipewyan and at first made very slow progress towards Fort McPherson. The late spring was the problem. In a letter of 24 May to Lady Lonsdale he wrote:

> It began to snow and rain and blow very heavily so I borrowed an ox and a cart from an Indian. Put my bags bed etc on it and I started off at 4 to cross the *portage* [a 16 mile-long overland section around a series of rapids] with a boy to show the way. It was a terrible road. We stuck in the mud several times and it took me seven and a half hours hard work to reach the fort [Fort

Smith]. There I found no food of any sort or kind, no flour tea or fish, so I had to go to bed the first time for 3 days wet, tired and foodless.

By early June there was no improvement and further *portages*, this time around fractured ice on the river, had to be negotiated. His journal records:

> 8 June: I had the men up at 6.00 and by 1.00 we had our boat over the ice and reloaded, only to be stopped again at 2.00 by 200 yards of jammed ice. 10 June: The men were got up with difficulty at 7 A.M. & a wet hard mornings work was before, as portaging 2837 lbs for 200 yards... . 11 June: ...the mosquitoes were fearful. 12 June: This is the hardest & most disagreeable work that I have ever done, & shall be glad when it is over.

In letters to Lady Lonsdale he sounds increasingly sorry for himself: 'I don't think this country has anything in the world to recommend it, and certainly there is no sport so far worth coming for at all. Moose shooting is a very overrated sport not half as much fun as stalking or shooting deer in the park at home'. He wrote about her coming out to join him when he got back to Winnipeg and then returning via Japan and India which would enable him to shoot elephants. He told her that 'I have some nice furs for you but there is a terrible scarcity'. He blamed others for the shortage of game to shoot: 'All the traders tell me that the Indians kill everything in such a wanton way that soon there will be nothing but fish left'.

By July travelling was easier, and once on the Mackenzie River, Lonsdale could sail and row down river to Fort Simpson where he was able to board *Wrigley*, the steamboat that had the previous year begun plying the northern reaches of the river system during the summer months. In the next few days he travelled several hundreds of miles as far as Fort McPherson on the Peel River. Once established there he wrote to Lady Lonsdale explaining that he was sending some of what he had collected back south on board *Wrigley*: 'I am sending out two beautiful musk ox heads', and 'I have...quite a museum of Indian works, & I am sending out a pair of Hunting and Tracking snow shoes from all different tribes where the patern differ, which varie from 7 feet long to 2 feet'(*sic*). Some animal trophies were acquired through purchase rather than by hunting, and the ethnographic artefacts, collected without any record-keeping, were acquired through gifts or by purchase.

Lonsdale spent almost seven weeks at Fort McPherson. Twelve of the days were taken up by a journey to Liverpool Bay on the Beaufort Sea. It was arranged in order to provide him with an opportunity to hunt Arctic animals, but it is best remembered for the time he spent with the Mackenzie Eskimo. Sir John Richardson had been one of the few earlier visitors to report on this ethnic group so what Lonsdale wrote has considerable value since he arrived just before white incomers changed these people for ever. In 1888 the Mackenzie Eskimo had a fierce reputation as they had little time for outsiders. Lonsdale was accompanied by two Englishmen, eight Indians and two Eskimos, and he was able to reveal his innate self-confidence when he wrote to his wife: 'From all accounts we shall not return alive...but personally I have not the faintest idea of any reason for what is called fear'.

The most memorable event during this journey was his observation of a beluga hunt. The beluga (*Delphinapterus leucas*) is sometimes known as the white whale. In a long letter to Lord Worcester written on his return to Fort McPherson, Lord Lonsdale began:

> Having safely returned from the sea coast and the wild inhabitants living on its shore, I thought you might like to hear an account of our proceedings since I last wrote to you. I often think how this month last year we were enjoying ourselves on Shap Fells, and I very much miss the grouse lets which next to the hunting I enjoy shooting more than anything else. However I kept up the 12th of August by shooting 6 brace of Arctic grouse, some Rock Ptarmigan and golden plovers, and thought of you while so occupied.

He went on to describe the beluga hunt:

> 50 kiacks [kayaks] with one man in each came out [from the shore] with harpoons attached by long lines to big [seal] bladders full of air. Every man was tied into his kiack & a waterproof skin sewn on him. We now reached the outpost men & waited for the remainder. They soon came 84 in all...forming a semicircle 3 miles wide and advanced behind the whales splashing & hooting. We soon saw they had 11 whales ahead, & they drove them into shallow water. Then the nearer man to each [whale] made a sprint & harpooned the one nearest him, some [kayakers] turning completely over in the operation & back as quick as lightening. Then you saw nothing but spouting. A spear with bladder attached went into them until they had killed ten. Now they called & 24 Omeacks [umiaks], 2 wives in each, came rowing out. They came in pairs alongside the whale & took out the Harpoons, Spears etc handing them each to the owners whom they knew by the mark on the spear. They insert a wooden blow pipe and fill the wound with air, tieing the skin tight. This floats the whale high, and after attaching him to the stern of the Omeacks, one kiack attached also on either side, they made it a procession home, singing all the way and talking over the hunt. By the time we arrived home it was 1 A.M. & all retired to their respective

dwellings, skin tents for the most part, tying the whales to poles placed in the bay for that purpose to await the later hours of the day before being skinned & cut up.

However the day was not yet over for Lonsdale:

> I now thought I had had a longish day & was walking home when I espied a man watching me from behind his door with a big knife in his hand. I had not set eyes on his villainous countenance before & seeing as I thought he meant mischief, I walked boldly up to his door, threw it open & walked in. He immediately made one spring at me, & a stab with his knife, only to find himself reclining in the corner of his house, his nose having come violently in the way of my left. I pulled out my revolver & showed it to him, sat down, lit my pipe and offered him a piece of tobacco.

Stories such as this and his later claim, for which there is no evidence, that he reached Banks Island, considerably nearer the North Pole, compromised his real achievements in the popular imagination.

His visit to Liverpool Bay enabled him to further supplement his artefact collection with gifts made to him: 'Kagley [the chief] gave me a Kiack complete with Harpoon, knives etc. etc. just ready for whaling'.

On 7 September Lonsdale left Fort McPherson on the longest stage of his journey, but by this time he was losing interest and the journal and letters are less informative. Initially his route was overland to the upper reaches of the Yukon River. He then followed the river to Russian Mission, the headquarters in Alaska of the Russian Orthodox Church. Despite travelling as fast as was possible, passing through an area of recent gold strikes (he was later to claim in *The People* in 1936 that his discoveries of gold had prompted the Klondike Gold Rush), winter caught up with him, and it was obvious that there would be no further ships leaving Alaska for the south in 1888. He remained at Russian Mission for six weeks before setting out for Kodiak in the depths of winter. He passed the Russian Christmas in the raucous surroundings of the cosmopolitan population of the Nushagak trading post. The route to Katmai (on the way to Kodiak) was followed across very difficult terrain in appalling weather; Lonsdale claimed that he had to push his team of Indians to the limit. On 12 February 1889 he reached Katmai, but had to wait until 19 March to cross to Kodiak Island, and until mid-April to board a steamer to San Francisco where he arrived on 23 April. He never returned to the Arctic.

So what did the Yellow Earl achieve? The newspapers of the time were undecided. *The San Francisco Daily Examiner* called his adventure a 'remarkable Arctic journey [that] has attracted the attention of the whole civilized world'. A New York newspaper described how 'the members of the Royal Geographical Society [of London] are laughing at Lord Lonsdale's claims to have done something good in the way of geographical discovery. The assertion that he has discovered anything worth knowing, or has gained any information which will be of value to scientific men, is treated as a huge joke'. The *Illustrated London News* described his journey as 'an enterprising and courageous performance'. One reporter suggested that Lonsdale's greatest achievement was his self-discovery that 'he had enough pluck to go'. Despite the hyperbole, there was some element of truth in all these observations.

He achieved his sporting objectives in that Lowther Castle was embellished with sporting trophies as well as curios that he had collected on his journey. Many of these items remained at Lowther until the auction of the contents of the castle which was held in 1947. Amongst the polar objects which were sold were polar bear, musk ox and husky skin rugs, twenty-one pairs of snow shoes, two kayaks and three arctic sledges. Although he added little to geographical or scientific knowledge, the two-hundred ethnographic artefacts made up largely of tools, hunting equipment (Figure 6.5), clothing (Figure 6.6) ritual items (Figure 6.7), domestic utensils, and curios made as souvenirs for the non-native market (Figure 6.8) that he presented to the

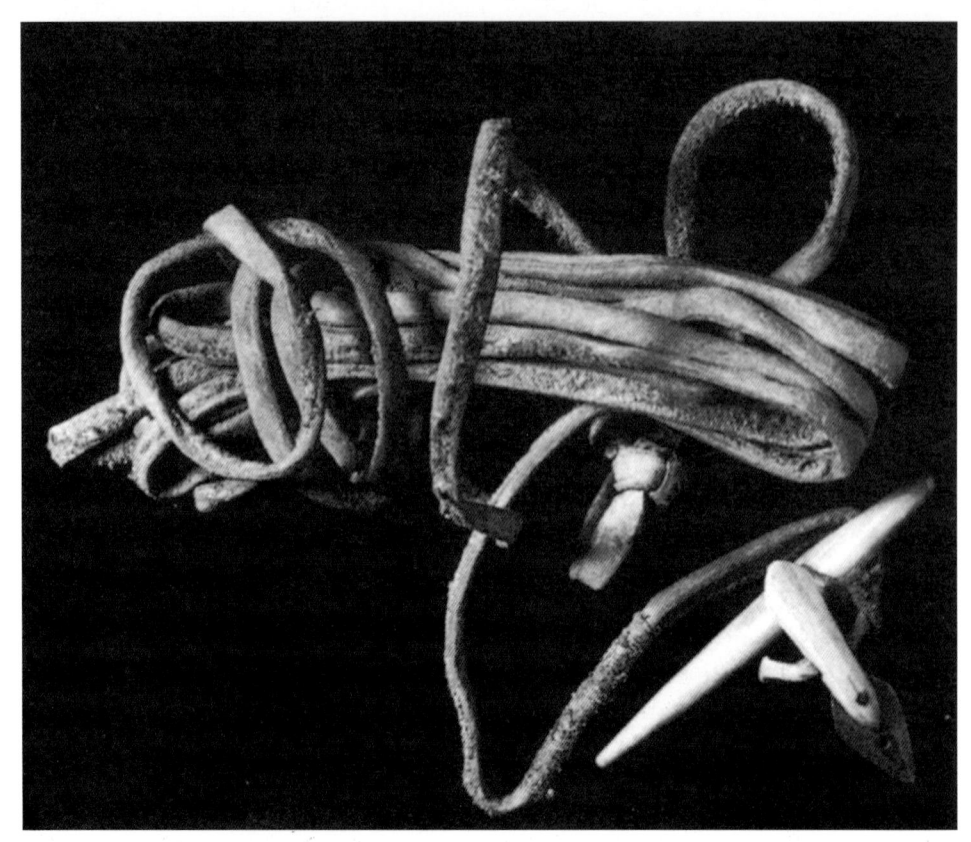

Figure 6.5. Eskimo-Aleut Harpoon-head and line made of steel, ivory, cord, horn and hide(?). *(© Trustees of the British Museum)*

Figure 6.6. Gauntlets made of skin (fish, salmon?), grass and hide: South-West Alaska Eskimos.
(© Trustees of the British Museum)

British Museum was a collection of considerable importance made more so by the archive that accompanied it, even though the detailed contextualised information that ethnographers would have wished for is missing. As the first Arctic collection presented to the museum by a private traveller, it may have acted as an encouragement to later adventurers to do the same. His description of the beluga hunt with the Mackenzie Eskimos remains an important description of their traditional hunting methods. Lonsdale embarked upon a real adventure by choosing not to follow in the footsteps of other independent travellers who in the 1880s were more likely to visit the tropics. Although he took some rudimentary maps, there were neither guidebooks nor basic facilities beyond those available to those who worked in the area. It is probably fair to say that few people with the means to do it would have considered making such an arduous journey at that time. His

Figure 6.7. A Pacific Eskimo mask made of wood, feathers and quills, probably collected in Alaska. *(© Trustees of the British Museum)*

journey did allow him to remove himself from the limelight, and by the time of his return to San Francisco the press had become more interested in what he had been doing than in the scandal that had sent him to the Arctic in the first place. On his return there did seem to be some reconciliation with his wife, Lady Grace Cicelie, since she travelled to the United States to meet him. Much later in 1938 they celebrated their sixtieth wedding anniversary with some splendour.

Figure 6.8. Model Umiak or boat with five figures (a women's boat) made of skin, wood, wool and down, probably purchased in Alaska. *(© Trustees of the British Museum)*

Lonsdale was not an explorer in the tradition of earlier eras. His significance, apart from his recording of his observations of the Mackenzie Eskimos and his gift to the British Museum, lies in how he used the Arctic as a place for 'sport and pleasure'. In that, he was in the vanguard of a new type of moneyed traveller who saw the Arctic as a playground that provided exciting and different opportunities for adventure. Clive Holland's definitive listing of Arctic expeditions hardly refers to 'sporting' or tourist ventures prior to that of Lonsdale's. In 1888, as well as Lonsdale's expedition, there were three sporting expeditions to Spitsbergen and an art expedition to Greenland. In the decade following his return in 1889 there were almost annual 'tourist' cruises to Spitsbergen where the infrastructure included, from 1896, a Norwegian-built hotel designed to accommodate the growing number of visitors. In addition there were eighteen other sporting, 'tourist', painting and mountaineering expeditions to an increasingly diverse range of Arctic destinations including a considerable number to the Mackenzie River basin. While still in Winnipeg before leaving for the north, he wrote in his journal: 'I hope I shall have some fun, they think it is a dangerous journey and that I cannot do it – But I shall! They don't think I can do the 1st part but I will and the 2nd part – 3rd – and 4th and bring lots of heads and skins back'. Lonsdale proved that it was possible to travel, even unprepared, through the Arctic, enjoy yourself and survive, and in that lies his importance.

★ ★ ★ ★ ★

S∪GGESTED F∪RTHER READING

R. David, 'Hugh Lowther, Fifth Earl of Lonsdale, in the Arctic: Explorer-Scientist, Sportsman, Traveller or Tourist?', *Transactions of the Cumberland and Westmorland Antiquarian and Archaeological Society*, Third Series, Vol. III, 2003, 185-201.

L. Dawson, *Lonsdale*, (London, Odhams, 1946).

S. Krech, *A Victorian Earl in the Arctic*, (London, British Museum, 1989).

D. Sutherland, *The Yellow Earl: The Life of Hugh Lowther Fifth Earl of Lonsdale, 1857-1944* (London, Cassell, 1965).

Chapter 7
'An intellectual entertainment for intellectual people':
The Rural Imagination and the Arctic

During the nineteenth century there was a substantial increase in the number and variety of texts, images and imaginings jostling for the attention of the public. Many of the more dramatic representations such as panoramas, pantomimes, *tableaux vivants*, and paintings and photographs which were exhibited in national and international exhibitions were only readily available to urban populations. However, before 1851 over 50% of the population of the United Kingdom lived outside urban areas, and throughout the century these communities would have had access to some of the descriptions of the Arctic and accounts of exploration through books, newspapers and magazines. They would also have seen visual representations of the Arctic in the travelogues of the explorers, illustrations in juvenile literature and some popular magazines, and on disposable items such as biscuit tins and cigarette cards. As Cumbrian communities became less remote, the Arctic seems to have attained a surprisingly high profile - high enough for the vicar of Edenhall, near Penrith, on hearing the story of the fate of Franklin as reported by Captain McClintock on his return with the evidence on 21 September (1859), to be moved to write a poem: 'The lament of the last man, on his way to the Great Fish River'. Within five days the poem (Appendix 2) was completed, and it was published in the *Carlisle Journal* on 30 September, thus demonstrating the speed at which news about the Arctic could spread to, and from, the most rural of parishes. So, what factors enabled the Arctic to become a topic of local interest? What texts, images and imaginings were available to a rural population; what access did they have to them; and what would these people have understood about the Arctic from them?

For some Cumbrians, their communities included people with direct knowledge of the Arctic. Skeffington Lutwidge, Sir John Richardson, the Yellow Earl and the Whitehaven whaling community all had experience of the Arctic and on their return to Cumbria lived amongst people with whom they no doubt shared at least some of their experiences. They brought stories of the Arctic, filtered through their own experiences and memories, directly to the drawing rooms, reading rooms and public houses of Cumbria. The more exotic or immediate the experience the greater would have been its appeal. In 1774 the 24 Whitehaven mariners on board the Liverpool whaleship *Golden Lion* had first-hand experiences of meeting Greenlanders to recount to their friends and family back in Cumbria. From 7 April *Golden Lion* and *Hope* of Whitby were in company on the west coast of Greenland. In his journal Thomas Atkinson, the surgeon in *Hope,* describes how on Sunday 17th April both he and Robert Peacock, the master of *Hope,* 'went on board the Golden Lion Captain Thompson'. He describes how 'two Indians [Greenlanders] in their Canoes had left the Ships Side [Hope] before we got on board' and that 'before we return'd to our vessel again, they had visited our people and left them likewise'. Such 'fraternisation' no doubt became the basis of stories told back home, and may have resulted in the sailors' acquisition of native artefacts which would eventually find their way into museum collections. Atkinson went on to write:

> As soon as they got along side they called out for a Pipe and Toobac (as they call Tobacco) with which our people soon accommodated them, and gave them Biscuits, Pork etc all which they received with seeming great thankfulness, and as much Complaisences as they were Masters of.

For both whalers and explorers contact with the native people was always an interesting experience and often recounted at length in their journals.

During the autumn of 1860 William Jones, the dog-driver on McClintock's expedition, gave a public lecture at Ulverston which apparently came alive when he departed from his script and told of first-hand experiences. Despite 'being rather timid in delivering his maiden lecture' he began by describing the events of the expedition from fitting out in Aberdeen to the discovery by four of the crew, of which he was one, of the 'remains of Sir John Franklin's expedition', presumably the document found in the cairn at Point Victory. The reporter from the *Ulverston Advertiser* commented that towards the end Jones 'laid aside his manuscript and told a plain straightforward tale…speaking of icebergs, whales, polar bears, the dresses worn, the food consumed, and the general habits observed, in the Arctic Regions'. Despite the audience being unable 'to catch all he said', his real-life experiences clearly brought an immediacy to his story.

As well as these few people with first-hand experience of the Arctic, there were also people living in, or visiting, Cumbria who were related to some of the great polar explorers of the nineteenth century. For example, during the 1830s a frequent visitor to Mirehouse, the home of his friend James Spedding, was Alfred, Lord Tennyson. When in 1850 he married Emily Sellwood, the niece of Sir John Franklin, their arrival at Mirehouse for part of their honeymoon at the very time when the country was following the progress of the numerous search expeditions, ensured that the developing story surrounding the fate of Franklin had a particular resonance in the Lake District. Sixty years later, in 1910 Sir Ernest Shackleton, the Antarctic explorer, gave a lecture in Carlisle and began by remarking that his audience included Canon Rawnsley, a grand-nephew of Sir John Franklin, Anne Barker, the wife of the Dean of Carlisle, who was the daughter of Sir James Clark Ross, and Canon A. G. Loftie, vicar of Wetheral and honorary canon of Carlisle Cathedral, who was a nephew of Captain Crozier who had accompanied both Franklin and Ross on voyages of Arctic exploration. All these people would no doubt have talked about their distinguished friends and ancestors, and their houses may have contained some inherited mementoes of Arctic explorations.

In some cases communities continued to be reminded of their link with the Arctic long after the people who had travelled there had died. The memorials erected in churches to the memory of some of these adventurers highlighted their polar activities. Such was the case with the plaques erected to the memory of Skeffington Lutwidge at Irton church (Figure 2.15) which drew attention to his command of HMS *Carcass* 'On a Voyage of Discovery Towards the North Pole', and to the memory of Sir John Richardson, 'the Constant Companion of Sir John Franklin in Arctic Exploration' at Grasmere church (Figure 5.8). Unfortunately neither incorporated any polar iconography therefore denying the local population a further opportunity to imagine the landscapes and seascapes through which the Arctic explorers travelled. However, the significance of these memorials as witness to polar deeds should not be exaggerated. It is clear that just because a memorial exists it does not mean that it was even noticed or viewed through 'a polar lens'. For example in 1842, having stood in front of the Lutwidge memorial, Samuel Jefferson, a local antiquary, wrote:

> At the head of the family pew of the Lutwidges, is a monument remarkably chaste and classical in its design, elegant and masterly in its execution, imposing by its height and the richness and dazzling polish of the materials, but above all, fascinating for the studied correctness and laboured finish of its minutest detail; in fact one of those splendid specimens of art to which the eye of the connoisseur may revert again and again, and still find something new to admire and applaud.

Readers of his book were encouraged to approach the memorial as a work of art and craftsmanship rather than from the perspective of Lutwidge as a person or an interest in his career. At Grasmere it was the memorial to William Wordsworth rather than that to Sir John Richardson which was described at length in every guide book to the Lake District.

The most dramatic of the Cumbrian memorials was that raised in memory of Sir John Barrow at Ulverston (Figure 5.3). The memorial on

Hoad Hill was designed as a seamark and therefore intended to be useful. It was based upon the shape of the Eddystone Lighthouse, but incorporated no iconography, Arctic or otherwise. The fact that it was paid for by 'the great and the good' of the United Kingdom including practically every Arctic explorer of note ensured that at the time of the laying of its foundation stone in 1850 (Figure 5.5), there was widespread press coverage which gave an opportunity to recount the events of Sir John's life and his interest in Arctic exploration. This did much to promote the accomplishments of the Arctic explorers in the Ulverston community.

The Arctic was also kept in the public eye through the creation and exhibition of paintings and portraits, the carving of inscriptions and the display of artefacts associated with the region. Equally significant were the writing of travelogues and histories, and the use of Arctic imagery in the writings of poets. Even the largely imaginary Arctic that appeared on disposable objects such as the Carlisle-manufactured biscuit tins and F. and J. Smith's cigarette cards played their part. The fact that Cumbrian writers, craftsmen, designers and tradesmen drew upon the Arctic in so many ways demonstrates the extent to which its landscapes and exploration had penetrated their consciousness.

Some paintings had wide public impact; others could only be seen by the elite for whom they had been created. Of the former the most significant by far was the arrival of Rignold's 'Panorama of the Arctic Regions' at the Young Men's Christian Association Hall in Fisher Street, Carlisle during the summer of 1876. Its appearance in Carlisle was part of a nationwide tour which included Shrewsbury (Figure 7.1). It consisted of a moving panorama of vast canvases which was unrolled in front of the paying audience. Rignold's slogan, 'An intellectual entertainment for intellectual people', reflects the panorama's role as both entertainment and education. The pictures were imaginings – images of the Arctic mediated by artists who were themselves reliant on other images brought back by explorers, in this case 'Captains Ross and Parry'. The publicity stretched credibility through suggesting that the pictures had been painted by J.M.W. Turner, even though Turner had died a quarter of a century earlier in 1851. Despite this, the entertainment was popular. According to the *Carlisle Journal* Mr Rignold, the owner and manager, with the aid of a map gave 'a very interesting lecture' on Arctic expeditions from the sixteenth century to that of Sir George Nares who was at that time in the Arctic. The performance was designed to replicate the sights and events of a typical expedition to the Arctic. As the reviewer in the *Carlisle Journal* wrote:

> No one expedition is specifically followed, but we have representations of icebergs and ice-floes, encounters with whales and bears, the piloting of the vessels through the ice, preparations

Figure 7.1. The poster for Rignold's *Panorama of the Arctic Regions* which was shown at Shrewsbury, 16 October 1876. Neither posters nor handbills have survived for the Carlisle event. Shropshire Archives 665/4/521 *(reproduced by courtesy of Shropshire Archives)*

for wintering in the ice-bound regions, the training of sledge parties, the occupation of the explorers during the long night of from four to six months, and the natural phenomena of the region, which are common to polar expeditions in general.

By 1876 much of this would have been reasonably familiar to many in the audience, but its scale would have been awe inspiring, and the way in which Mr Rignold incorporated his doubts as to the likely success of the Nares expedition would have made the entertainment more relevant and reminded the audience of the dangers. The paper recommended the panorama as 'a very pleasant and profitable way of spending a couple of hours'. For those who saw it, this panorama would almost certainly have had a dramatic impact on how they imagined the Arctic.

In contrast the two paintings (Figures 3.2 and 3.3) which have hung on the walls of the Spedding family home at Mirehouse for over two centuries would not have been seen by a wide audience. These too are imaginings which were possibly painted in Liverpool, the home port of *Neptune*, the ship depicted. In one painting *Neptune* is shown having considerable success during her 1778 voyage to the Greenland Sea, and in the other she is painted at the moment of sinking after being 'nipped' by the ice. The artist is unknown but was clearly familiar with this genre of painting, and with whaling and the Arctic environment. Those members of the family, their servants and friends who saw these paintings would have absorbed a spirited vision of the activities associated with whaling and the Arctic seascape, even if they would have acquired rather odd impressions of the hunt, with whales seemingly queuing up to be harpooned, and of the sinking of the vessel in what appears to be a holiday atmosphere as the crew on the ice await rescue.

Name recognition would have been important in the decisions of portraitists to paint and exhibit portraits of Arctic explorers. Some portraits, such as that of Dr John Richardson by R. Phillips RA, could be viewed by the public at an exhibition at the Carlisle Academy in 1825. Despite the reviewer from the *Carlisle Journal* writing that 'the dignified mien, so peculiar to the Doctor, is here accurately portrayed', for most people who saw it, Richardson would be relatively unknown. He did not come to live in Cumbria for another thirty years. Other portraits would have been seen by fewer people. The mural of Sir William Edward Parry at Crosthwaite, near Kendal, is one such example (Figure 5.9). Richard Cartmell's decision to paint Parry must have been the consequence of the latter's' high profile. Cartmell's pictures were usually of local worthies but his mural reveals the profile of the Arctic even in an out-of-the-way community in northern England. That Parry was a household name is further demonstrated by the engraver of the inscriptions at Ecclerigg (Figure 5.12). A local stonemason, William Longmire of Troutbeck, may have been the carver of the inscriptions, and the fact that Parry appears alongside Ross

Figure 7.2. A whalebone arch near Burneside in the early twentieth century *(reproduced by courtesy of Cumbria County Council, Carlisle Library)*

(Figure 5.13) and an eclectic mix of politicians, philanthropists, scientists and even a slave trader, demonstrates the extent to which Arctic explorers' names were known.

Interest in the Arctic would have been further stimulated by opportunities to view artefacts of polar exploration and objects acquired from the indigenous cultures. The memory of whaling was perpetuated through whalebone arches. At one time there were a number in the county. Sir John Barrow erected one in the Ulverston area, there was another at Gamblesby and a third, the only survivor, near Staveley (Figures 7.2 and A2). Peter Crosthwaite's museum in Keswick displayed 'the Horn of the Sea Unicorn' and 'the Skin of an Immense White Bear from Greenland' presented by the owners of the Whitehaven whaling ship *Precedent*, alongside a collection of various body parts of whales, walruses and bears (Figure 7.3). It also had a variety of Inuit artefacts presumably acquired by explorers or missionaries in Greenland and around Baffin Bay, although some may have come from the whalers. These included a 'small basket made of birch bark', a pair of 'Esquimaux indian boots made of seal skin', a 'Model of an Esquimaux indian's canoe, with the representation of the inhabitants and their mode of travelling', and 'a Greenland Lady's Dress made of Seal Skin' donated by a Mrs Slater of Liverpool. The long-abandoned Museum of Cumberland at Distington displayed a similar range of material which included a collection of whalebones attached to an exterior wall. The Museum of the Kendal

> **The Horn of the Sea Unicorn**, being the horn of a fish taken in the Greenland Seas. This horn measures 5 feet 8½ inches, and was presented to this museum by the owner of a vessel called the President, belonging to Whitehaven
>
> **The Skin of an immense White Bear from Greenland**, it was presented to this museum by the owners of a vessel called the President of Whitehaven

Figure 7.3. Extracts from the catalogue of Peter Crosthwaite's museum, Keswick, (no date) *(reproduced by courtesy of Cumbria County Council, Kendal Library)*

Vestibule Leading to Room No. 5.

1 Guayaquil Hammock
2 A Dress made of grass, worn as armour by the natives of the North Seas
3 Pair of Ancient Boots, from Ashlick Hall, near Ulverstone
4 Pair of Boots, from the North Seas
5 Carved Wood, from Grasmere Church
6 Monumental Card of Dr. Archer, of Oxenholme
7 Skin of a Boa Constrictor
8 Skin of a Bear, said to have been killed by Lord Nelson when a midshipman
9 Portrait of a Duke of Cumberland

Figure 7.4. From the Catalogue of Museum of the Kendal Literary and Scientific Society, 1870 *(reproduced by courtesy of Cumbria County Council, Kendal Library)*

Literary and Scientific Society made a bold claim for one of its star exhibits (Figure 7.4). It advertised that visitors could view the 'skin of a Bear, said to have been killed by Lord Nelson when a midshipman'. Clearly the museum was tempted into making a convenient, but erroneous, connection which attempted to capitalise on Robert Southey's story of Nelson's encounter with the bear in his *The Life of Nelson* and on the county's links with his commander Skeffington Lutwidge.

Although few people beyond the friends of Lord Lonsdale and his servants had an opportunity to view the trophies and artefacts on the walls of Lowther Castle, loan exhibitions, supported by the Earl and held in towns around the county, enabled some of the artefacts that he brought back from the Arctic to be more widely viewed. For example in Kirkby Stephen in the 1890s items loaned by Lord Lonsdale included 'a polar bear skin and head', 'an Esquimaux Lady's suit in five pieces', 'a musk ox skin and head', 'Two pair snow shoes', and 'an Esquimaux Dog harness'. Although exhibits are often viewed as objects which connect the viewer directly with the 'Other', how they were understood depends on how they were displayed in the museums and at the loan exhibitions. Cumbria's museums, as well as the loan collections, were 'cabinets of curiosities' - unsystematic displays of often personal collections, where the artefacts were accompanied by limited, and possibly erroneous, information.

Books provided another opportunity for at least the literate population of Cumbria to become acquainted with the Arctic. The county's adult population was unusually literate in the nineteenth century; it has been estimated that about 82% of men and 76% of women could read and write. Books were expensive but book society and library membership made available large numbers of volumes at a very reasonable cost. Even in 1828, its first year, Ambleside Book Society had 28 members. As subscription libraries multiplied, the number of adults who were members and could acquire their books increased.

Those that joined subscription libraries were often able to borrow a good range of books on Arctic exploration. For example in 1838 Kendal Subscription Library had books by Ross, Parry, Franklin and Scoresby; Whitehaven Subscription Library had a similar set of books in 1851; and Keswick Library in 1882 listed John Rae's *Arctic Expeditions 1829-33*, Franklin's *Journey to the Polar Sea*, Nordenskiold's *Arctic Voyages 1858-79*, and Sir John Richardson's *Journal of a Boat Voyage in the Arctic Searching Expedition*. Even a small village lending library, such as that at Levens, had one book on North West Passage exploration. The development of libraries in connection with working men's institutes further extended the readership of books. Kendal's working men's institute in 1881 had a book by Sir John Ross.

With an annual subscription individuals could subscribe directly to the national circulating libraries, such as Mudie's (from 1842) and W.H. Smith's (from 1860), or they could gain access to these libraries through membership of some local lending libraries. For example members of the library of the Literary and Scientific Institution of Kendal also had access to Mudie's. In 1860, just after the era of the Franklin search expeditions had given prominence to Arctic exploration, Mudie's had copies of books written by a range of Arctic explorers – Sir John Richardson, Sir William Edward Parry, Captain McClintock, and Sherard Osborn, as well as books describing Arctic exploration such as J. Brown's *Expeditions in Search of Sir John Franklin*. These would have complemented the Literary and Scientific Institution of Kendal's own library which had volumes by Sir John Franklin, Dr. William Scoresby, and Sir John Ross as well as the very popular *Polar World*, by Dr. G. Hartwig. In Carlisle there were also some local circulating libraries such as I. F. Whitridge's Select Circulating Library which had a single volume on the North West Passage by Sir John Ross in 1845.

Private individuals had their own libraries. The largest libraries, such as that at Lowther Castle, had copies of numerous books on Arctic travel by Sir William Edward Parry, Sir John Ross, Sir John Franklin and Sir George Back, as well as the volumes of Hans Egede's *A Description of Greenland*. The sale catalogues of smaller libraries reveal fewer Arctic books. The library at Crag Brow, Windermere had a single volume by William Scoresby in 1855, and that of the Rev. Joseph Milner, Vicar of St Lawrence, Appleby, included only David Crantz's *History of Greenland*, which with its focus on the Moravian missionaries would have been of particular interest to a vicar.

Books written by explorers with a connection to Cumbria were more likely to be noticed. Of the Arctic explorers, Sir John Richardson was the most prolific author and wrote his last work, *The Polar Regions*, while

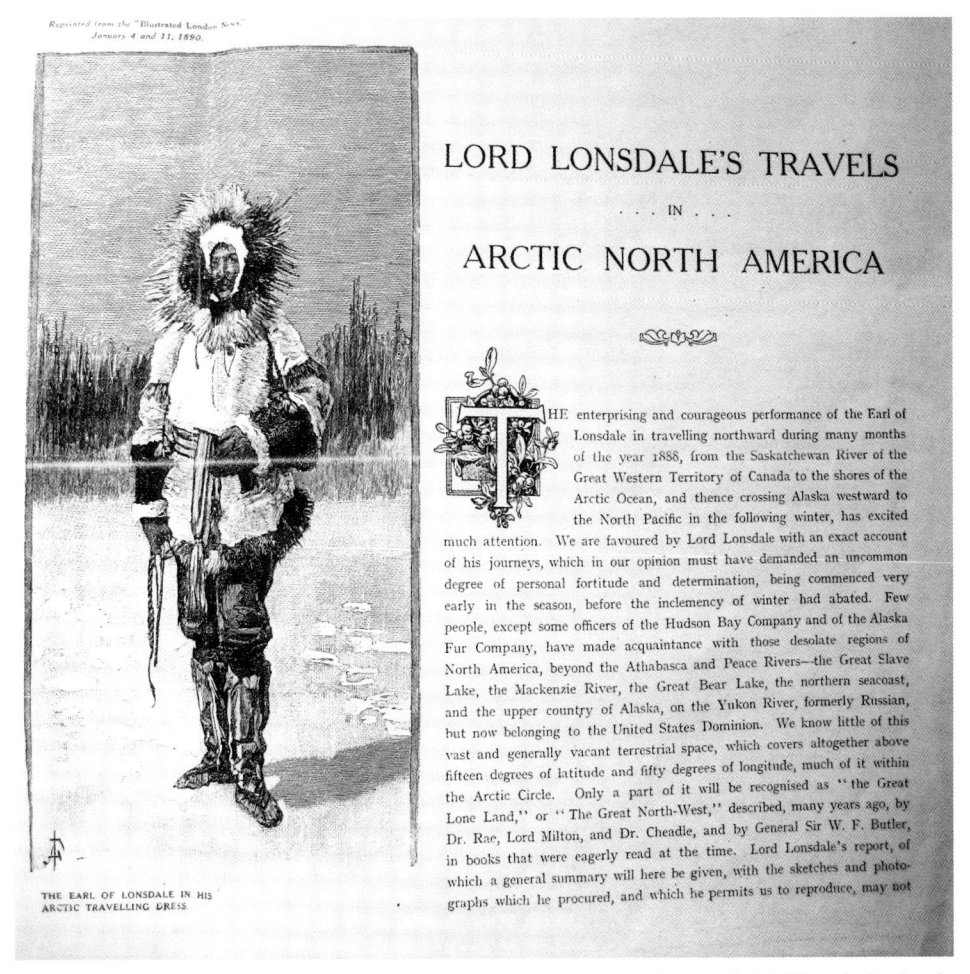

Figure 7.5. Part of the first of two instalments describing 'Lord Lonsdale's Travels in Arctic North America' that appeared in the *Illustrated London News*, 4 January, 1890.

at Grasmere. As the Yellow Earl did not write a published account of his journey, the public had to make do with a variety of newspaper articles, the most significant of which appeared in the *Illustrated London News* in 1890 (Figure 7.5). Sir John Barrow wrote copiously, but his most significant volume on Arctic exploration, *A Chronological History of Voyages into the Arctic Regions*, was originally published at the beginning of the revival of interest in the North West Passage in 1818, well after his childhood in Cumbria. It may well have been two of the 'Lake poets' who did most to promote the polar worlds amongst Cumbrians. When Samuel Taylor Coleridge came to live at Greta Hall, Keswick in the summer of 1800, *The Rime of the Ancient Mariner* was already popular, having been published in 1798. Coleridge was obviously familiar with the growing literature of Arctic exploration and it is therefore unsurprising that he drew on images of the Arctic 'sublime' in his writings. Although *The Rime of the Ancient Mariner* is located in the Antarctic region, many of Coleridge's sources - it has been suggested that he knew the accounts of Thomas James (1631-32) and Constantine Phipps (1773) - were descriptions of the Arctic. While Coleridge was at Christ's Hospital, he had been tutored by William Wales who had observed the transit of Venus in Hudson Bay (1768-69) and had accompanied Captain James Cook as astronomer on his second voyage from 1772 to 1775, during which the Antarctic Circle was crossed for the first time. Very probably Wales provided the young Coleridge with first-hand accounts of both polar worlds. In addition Coleridge's reading of two missionary works from Greenland – Hans Egede *A Description of Greenland* (1745) and David Crantz *The History of Greenland* (1767) – underpinned his 1796 poem *The Destiny of Nations: a Vision*. Although Coleridge only lived in the Lake District until 1804, his fame and connections ensured that his work was well represented in the libraries of Cumbria.

Coleridge's brother-in-law, Robert Southey, lived at Greta Hall between 1803 and his death in 1843 (Figure 7.6 and A5). While there he wrote *The Life of Nelson*, which incorporated the story of Nelson and the polar bear. This was the first biography to promote this story which additionally provided Skeffington Lutwidge and the 1773 expedition to the North Pole with further exposure to the reading public. Using a variety of sources Southey wrote a eulogy, published in 1813, that sought to show how events in Nelson's life contributed to the emergence of the national hero. Whether or not Nelson

Figure 7.6. An engraving of Greta Hall and Keswick Bridge by W. Westall/E. Francis. This engraving predates Southey's residence at Greta Hall as by the time he lived there the building had been enlarged *(reproduced by courtesy of Cumbria County Council, Carlisle Library)*

had an encounter with a polar bear in the way suggested, Southey's story demonstrated Nelson's leadership, his bravery verging on foolhardiness, and his tendency to ignore orders when it suited him. These were written up as evidence of traits in his character that were to make him the hero he later became.

The elderly Skeffington Lutwidge was living at Holmrook when Southey wrote his book. However, there does not seem to have been any contact between them, and Southey promoted the Nelson story at the expense of that of Lutwidge and even of Phipps, the commander of the expedition. Lutwidge did not mention Nelson in his journal, but Southey gave the midshipman a significant role throughout the period that the ships were beset in the ice north of Spitsbergen. Southey wrote: 'Young as he was, Nelson was appointed to command one of the boats which were sent out to explore a passage into the open water' and he went on to describe an episode where Nelson became involved in saving the crew of another boat from being attacked by a walrus. Southey continued:

> Young Nelson exposed himself in a more daring manner. One night during the mid-watch, he stole from the ship with one of his comrades…and set off over the ice in pursuit of a bear… [later] the two adventurers were seen, at a considerable distance from the ship, attacking a huge bear. The signal for them to return was immediately made; Nelson's comrade called upon him to obey it, but in vain; his musket had flashed in the pan, their ammunition was expended; and a chasm in the ice, which divided him from the bear, probably preserved his life. "Never mind," he cried; "do but let me get a blow at the devil with the butt-end of the musket, and we shall have him". Capt. Lutwidge, however seeing his danger, fired a gun, which had the desired effect of frightening the bear; and the boy then returned, somewhat afraid of the consequences of his trespass. The captain reprimanded him sternly for conduct so unworthy of the office which he filled, and desired to know what motive he could have for hunting a bear. "Sir…I wished to kill the bear, that I might carry the skin to my father".

The story was frequently illustrated, often with largely inaccurate pictures of polar bears or the Arctic landscape (Figure 2.10). According to Southey, Nelson was again placed in charge of a cutter when the boats were being hauled over the ice in order to find open water and a route back to land. He ensured that Nelson, rather than Skeffington Lutwidge, would be remembered by his readers, many of whom lived in the county. Southey became a key source for practically all subsequent biographers of Nelson, so for many people the story of Nelson and the bear, rather than the events of the 1773 voyage in general, came to represent the quintessential Arctic adventure.

As well as books, periodicals were a source of information on the Arctic. Some people took out personal subscriptions to one or more, but it was also possible to borrow them from the subscription and circulating libraries. Many subscribed to *Blackwood's Edinburgh Magazine*, the *Edinburgh Review* and the *Quarterly Review*. The library of the Literary and Scientific Institution of Kendal also took the *Cornhill Magazine* and *Macmillan's Magazine*, and the Ambleside Book Society additionally subscribed to *Frazer's London Magazine*, *Tait's Edinburgh Magazine* and the *New Monthly Review*. These periodicals regularly included features on Arctic exploration, wildlife and the living conditions and culture of the indigenous populations.

News from the Arctic was surprisingly easy to come by. Subscribers to *The Times* and other national papers were provided with information about the expeditions as soon as it became available – although of course it often had to await the return of the personnel to the United Kingdom or to places with telegraph communications. These articles were often reprinted *verbatim* in the regional and county press. During the 1820s the main Cumbrian newspapers such as the *Carlisle Journal*, the *Cumberland Paquet* and the *Westmorland Gazette* provided their readers with updates of Parry's various voyages and Franklin's overland expeditions in northern Canada. In the 1850s Cumbrians were kept in touch with news of the search expeditions for Sir John Franklin, and in 1859 the return of Captain Leopold McClintock with numerous relics and the answers to many of the questions about the fate of Franklin and his companions was recounted at length. The death of Lady Franklin in 1875 and the announcement of Nordenskiold's completion of the North-East Passage were both reported in the *Carlisle Journal*. Further information about the Arctic was provided through the printing of extracts from the published journals of Arctic explorers. The local newspapers printed extracts from Sir John Ross's *A Voyage of Discovery...in His Majesty's Ships Isabella and Alexander* within a few weeks of the book's appearance in 1819.

None of these articles was illustrated, so that readers had to rely on images seen elsewhere to help them appreciate the world which the explorers had penetrated. With the publication of the *Illustrated London News* (from 1842) and *The Graphic* (1869) along with other cheaper imitators, readers were provided with engravings which purported to illustrate the printed accounts. Although many originated in images created by personnel during the expeditions and were faithful attempts to render them into print, the opportunities for engravers to alter these images and add their own imaginings, or for editors to include pictures whose captions suggested that they illustrated what was being read, when clearly they did not, had the potential seriously to mislead the reader.

The illustrations to the two articles in the *Illustrated London News* which followed the Yellow Earl's return to the United Kingdom from Canada in 1889 demonstrate how the public could be misled. At that time it was not possible to reproduce photographs in mass-circulation magazines. Illustrations had to be engraved by engravers either working from their own imagination or from photographs, drawings or paintings provided for them. The engravers who worked on the two articles in the *Illustrated London News* used photographs provided by the Earl. Some engravings such as that of 'Fort Norman on the Mackenzie River' were based on photographs taken by Lonsdale on his journey and were accurate representations of the original image (Figure 7.7). However a number of the photographs had been taken in a photographer's studio in San Francisco on his way back to England, and when these were engraved, 'Arctic' backgrounds were invented by the engraver (Figures 7.8 and 7.9). In this case the engraving probably represents an attempt by the engraver to connect the Earl to a waterfall on the Hay River that he claimed to have discovered. Lonsdale's positioning in an Arctic landscape was a construction of the engraver, and the reader was given no hint that the picture was entirely created in San Francisco and London.

Figure 7.7. An engraving 'Fort Norman on the Mackenzie River' based on a Lonsdale photograph, *Illustrated London News*, 4 January, 1890.

Both the source of photographs and their captions had to be taken on trust. The engraving in figure 7.7 was based on a photograph taken by the Earl but some engravings that were used to illustrate the article came from photographs from other expeditions. Figure 7.10 is one of these and was faithfully engraved from the original photograph, but the caption 'A Noonday Halt. Temperature 55 Degrees below Zero', was added to illustrate a claim Lonsdale made about the severity of the weather. Figure 7.11 was also carefully engraved from a photograph and the correct caption used, but the scene depicted was several hundred miles from Lonsdale's route. The readers of the *Illustrated London News*, whether in Cumbria or elsewhere, would have had no means of distinguishing between those engravings which

Figure 7.8 A photograph of the Earl of Lonsdale in Arctic attire taken by I. W. Taber in San Francisco during his return journey in 1889 *(ownership lies with the Lowther Estate Trust)*

Figure 7.9 The engraving created from the photograph in Figure 7.9 which was published in the *Illustrated London News*, 11 January 1890.

Figure 7.10. 'A Noonday Halt. Temperature 55 Degrees below Zero', *Illustrated London News*, 11 January 1890.

Figure 7.11. 'York Factory, West Coast of Hudson's Bay', *Illustrated London News*, 4 January 1890.

were largely faithful reproductions of photographs that were taken on the journey, and pictures that originated elsewhere in Canada or even the San Francisco studio. They would also have had no means of verifying the authenticity of the captions.

Photographs from the Yellow Earl's journey were also made available to a wider audience as a set of magic lantern slides. It is not known whether these were solely shown to Lonsdale's guests at Lowther Castle or were shown more widely. However, any image-led presentation of the Earl's journey would have been dependent upon the images available. As with the *Illustrated London News* articles, the pictures came from many sources and any narrative that accompanied them may have included the imagined stories that were reproduced in the newspaper articles and biographies written later in his life.

Both estate staff and visitors who had access to the interior of Lowther Castle would not have been able to miss the mementoes of the Arctic that filled the building. In addition to other artefacts scattered around various rooms (Figure 7.12) the enormous entrance hall contained kayaks and a polar bear (Figure 7.13), and its walls were covered in the hunting trophies and snow shoes that the Yellow Earl had brought back.

Images of the Arctic had an even wider currency. Both the workforce at Hudson Scott's tin- plate factory in Carlisle and the purchasers of the thousands of Huntley and Palmer's 'Arctic' biscuit tins which were made there would have had their impression of the Arctic influenced by the pictures showing imaginary scenes from Arctic expeditions, including one which showed Arctic explorers sitting around a camp fire well supplied with Huntley and Palmer biscuits!

The evidence from Cumbria suggests that through people who had direct contact with the Arctic, some communities would have had opportunities to learn of the Arctic at first hand and been well aware of British activity there. The evidence of the Crosthwaite mural and the Ecclerigg inscriptions also suggests that people who could have had no direct contact with the Arctic or with people who were associated with the Arctic, were well aware of Arctic exploration and some of the key figures involved. A wider public had the opportunity to gain access to a variety of visual representations, and to see eclectic displays of artefacts. First-hand written accounts as well as the imaginings of poets and biographers extended still further the number of those who acquired at least some awareness of the Arctic environment, the

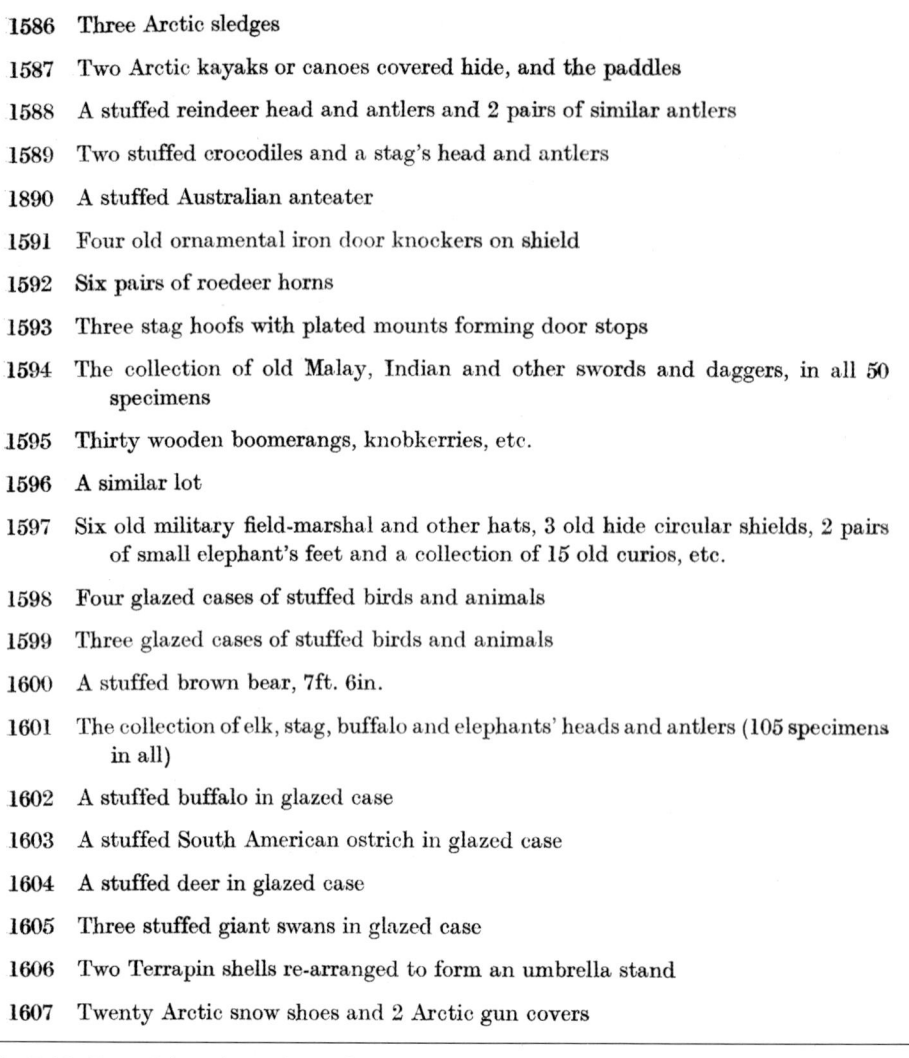

1586	Three Arctic sledges
1587	Two Arctic kayaks or canoes covered hide, and the paddles
1588	A stuffed reindeer head and antlers and 2 pairs of similar antlers
1589	Two stuffed crocodiles and a stag's head and antlers
1890	A stuffed Australian anteater
1591	Four old ornamental iron door knockers on shield
1592	Six pairs of roedeer horns
1593	Three stag hoofs with plated mounts forming door stops
1594	The collection of old Malay, Indian and other swords and daggers, in all 50 specimens
1595	Thirty wooden boomerangs, knobkerries, etc.
1596	A similar lot
1597	Six old military field-marshal and other hats, 3 old hide circular shields, 2 pairs of small elephant's feet and a collection of 15 old curios, etc.
1598	Four glazed cases of stuffed birds and animals
1599	Three glazed cases of stuffed birds and animals
1600	A stuffed brown bear, 7ft. 6in.
1601	The collection of elk, stag, buffalo and elephants' heads and antlers (105 specimens in all)
1602	A stuffed buffalo in glazed case
1603	A stuffed South American ostrich in glazed case
1604	A stuffed deer in glazed case
1605	Three stuffed giant swans in glazed case
1606	Two Terrapin shells re-arranged to form an umbrella stand
1607	Twenty Arctic snow shoes and 2 Arctic gun covers

Fig. 7.12. Part of the sale catalogue for the contents of Lowther Castle, 1947. Arctic artefacts jostle with items from around the world. *(reproduced by courtesy of Cumbria County Council, Carlisle Library)*

lives of the people who lived there, and the world of the explorers. That this was the case for Cumbria's intelligentsia is demonstrated by Harriet Martineau. Martineau, a political analyst, reformer and writer, was hardly a typical resident of Ambleside where she lived at The Knoll, but through her letters she shows that living in a Cumbrian village was no bar to being informed about polar exploration. She knew of Sir John Richardson at Grasmere, was aware of the Franklin search expeditions of Robert McClure and of the American Henry Grinnell, and she clearly knew Lady Jane Franklin, Sir John's wife, who gave her an inscribed copy of *Thirty Years in the Arctic Regions*, a narrative of Franklin's journeys, published in 1859. The extent to which this was true for the less educated Cumbrian is inevitably unclear.

Towards the end of the nineteenth century the activities of the Yellow Earl raised the profile of the Arctic (and himself) in the county, but the images that accompanied the promotion of his journey would have caused Cumbrians, as well as people beyond the county, considerable difficulties in distinguishing between a reality and a fiction. With less comparative material available, Cumbrians may have struggled more than their urban counterparts to recognise visual images of doubtful accuracy and the imaginative captions that sometimes accompanied them. However, it is clear that the Arctic had a high enough profile in Cumbria to allow many Cumbrians to imagine that very different world.

Figure 7.13. The polar bear killed by the Yellow Earl which was placed in the entrance hall of Lowther Castle. It was donated to Kendal Museum where it can still be seen. *(by courtesy of Kendal College. Photograph: Julian Sale)*.

★ ★ ★ ★ ★

SUGGESTED FURTHER READING

R. G. David, *The Arctic in the British Imagination*, (Manchester, Manchester University Press, 2000).

R. David, 'Hugh Lowther, Fifth Earl of Lonsdale, in the Arctic: Explorer-Scientist, Sportsman, Traveller or Tourist', *Transactions of the Cumberland and Westmorland Antiquarian and Archaeological Society*, Third Series, Vol. III, 2003, pp. 186-201.

R. A. Potter, *Arctic Spectacles: The Frozen North in Visual Culture, 1818-1875*, (Washington D.C., University of Washington Press, 2007).

Appendix 1
Places to visit in Cumbria

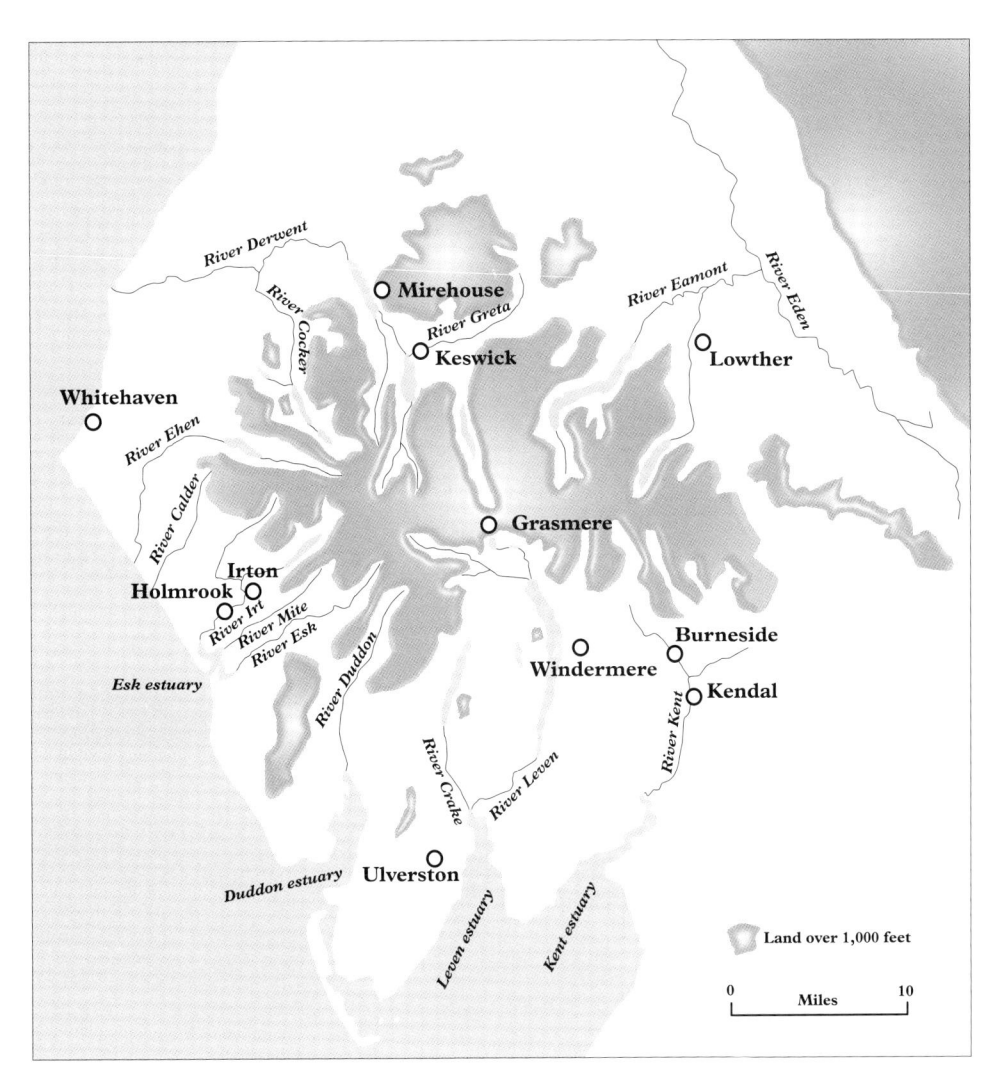

Figure A1. Map showing the location of the main places to visit in Cumbria

BASSENTHWAITE

The two paintings of the whale ship *Neptune* in 1778 (Figures 3.2 and 3.3) can be seen at Mirehouse. For details of opening times see: www.mirehouse.com

BURNESIDE

The only surviving (but rather dilapidated) whalebone arch in Cumbria can be seen over a gate to the left of the A591 when travelling from Kendal to Staveley (Figures 7.2 and A2). Its date and origin are uncertain.

Figure A2. The remains of the whalebone arch near Burneside. *(photograph: Rob David)*

GRASMERE

Sir John Richardson lived at Lancrigg from 1855 to 1865 (Figure 5.7). The house is now a guest house and various permissive footpaths open to the public wind through the estate. Some of the trees were almost certainly planted by Sir John, a keen gardener (www.lancrigg.co.uk). The parish church of St Oswald contains his memorial plaque which describes him as 'the constant companion of Sir John Franklin in Arctic exploration' (Figure 5.8).

HOLMROOK

Holmrook Hall, the home of Skeffington Lutwidge between about 1800 and his death in 1814, has been demolished (Figure 2.11). However, fragments of a gate (Figure A3), the stableyard (Figure 2.12) and outbuildings (Figure

A4) as well as the walled garden and gardener's cottage (Fig. 2.13) can be seen from a public right of way on the east side of the A595, north of the village of Holmrook.

Figure A3. The remains of the entrance to Holmrook Hall *(photograph: Rob David)*

Figure A4. Estate buildings at Holmrook Hall *(photograph: Rob David)*

Irton
The memorial to Skeffington Lutwidge is located in the parish church of St Paul (Figures 2.14 and 2.15). There are also a number of memorials to the Brocklebank family, shipbuilders of Whitehaven with interests in whaling.

Kendal
Two of the mammals brought back to Lowther Castle by the Yellow Earl can now be seen in Kendal Museum. They are a polar bear (Figure 7.14) and a juvenile musk ox. The polar bear said to have been brought back by Nelson is no longer there. For information on opening times see: www.kendalmuseum.org.uk. The British Museum in London usually has a number of artefacts from the collection donated by the Yellow Earl on display.

Keswick
Keswick Museum and Art Gallery replaced Peter Crosthwaite's private 'Museum or Cabinet of Curiosities' opened in 1781. That museum closed in 1870 and many original artefacts, including the Arctic ones, disappeared. The way the artefacts are displayed in the present museum to an extent reflects the cluttered appearance of Peter Crosthwaite's museum. For information on opening times see: www.keswickmuseum.webs.com Greta Hall (Figure A5), the home of Robert Southey, is now used for holiday accommodation but can be viewed from the approach road (www.gretahall.net).

Figure A5. Greta Hall, Keswick *(photograph: Rob David)*

Figure A6. The ruins of Lowther Castle *(photograph: Rob David)*

LOWTHER

The ruins of Lowther Castle, the home of the Fifth Earl of Lonsdale (The Yellow Earl) can be seen from public roads through Lowther Park (Figure A6). Both the castle and its gardens are currently being restored and in time further opportunities may exist for viewing the castle (www.lowthercastle.org). The surprisingly plain tomb of the Earl and his wife Cicelie (the 'My dearest Bod' of the letters from the Arctic) is located in the churchyard of the nearby St Michael's Church, Lowther (Figure A7). The archive of the Yellow Earl's journey to the Arctic is part of the Lowther Archive deposited at the Carlisle Archive Centre, Petterill Bank, Carlisle. Its reference is: DLONS/L/27.

Figure A7. The grave of the Yellow Earl and his wife Cicelie at Lowther Church *(photograph: Rob David)*

ULVERSTON

The cottage (a rare survival from the era) at Dragley Beck where Sir John Barrow was born and lived as a child can be seen from the Ulverston-Bardsea road (A5087) (Figure 5.2). For further information visit www.rootsweb.ancestry.com/~ukuhc/ The restored Hoad Monument, completed in 1851, can be viewed externally at any time. For details of opening hours contact: www.sirjohnbarrowmonument.co.uk (Figure 5.3).

WHITEHAVEN

There is surprisingly little to see at Whitehaven that can be directly connected to the ship-building or whaling industries. Much of the harbour layout as we see it today was completed by the mid-1780s. Many of the streets and Georgian town houses would have been familiar to the whalers and shipbuilders of the eighteenth century. The only house which can be connected to a person with interests in whaling is that of Captain Daniel Brocklebank (1741-1801) at No. 25 Roper Street (Figure 3.5). Around the marina are a number of seats designed as the lobes of a whale's tail. One has an inscription relating to the American John Paul Jones and his raid on Whitehaven in 1778 that resulted in the burning of *Thompson* which was later to become a whale ship. A visit to the shore at Parton, to the north of Whitehaven, might help a whaling enthusiast imagine the world of low-tech blubber-boiling for whale oil (Figure 3.7).

Figure A8. A general photograph of one of the inscribed slabs at Cragwood *(photograph: Maggie Sale)*

Windermere (Ecclerigg)

The rock inscriptions that include the names of Parry and Ross are located within the grounds of Cragwood Hotel at Ecclerigg on the A591 between Windermere and Ambleside (Figure A8, 5.12 and 5.13). Enquire at the hotel for permission and directions (www.lakedistrictcountryhotels.co.uk/cragwood-hotel).

Appendix 2

A poem by Beilby Porteus, Vicar of Edenhall from 1840 to 1870, published in the *Carlisle Journal*, 30 September 1859 p.6.

Figure A9. Photograph of Beilby Porteus *(reproduced by kind permission of the Church Wardens, PCC and Vicar of St. Cuthbert's Church, Edenhall)*

'SIR JOHN FRANKLIN'S ILL-FATED EXPEDITION'
THE LAMENT OF THE LAST MAN, ON HIS WAY TO THE GREAT FISH RIVER

They have fallen, one by one;
The last, but one, today –
God! Am I left alone,
To track this weary way;
My weary way to the River,
The haven where I would be?
But, alas, heart-struck I shiver –
I can never attain the sea!
I am touching his lifeless head,
A waif on this desolate shore;
I am kissing the last of the dead –
Shall I see man's face no more?
Cold, cold, cold;
But mine own hour not yet told!

In mine ear the terrible rush,
The thundering rush of the floe;
And the shriek of her ribs in the grinding crush,
And the good ship in her throe.
In mine heart, their mute despair
And the groans of our wailing knell,
As the death-call swoop'd thro' the pitiless air,
And the pale men droop'd and fell!
Where they fell they lay;
Not a knee rose more to the light;
The reeling and shrunken clay
Shrank at once into icy night!
Cold, cold, cold:
And mine hour as yet untold!

Mine eyelids burn: congeals
My brain within its cell,
And the scalding tear-drop steals
From an overflowing well;
For I dream of fond hearts at home,
I think of the brave that are gone;
As I gaze at this star-lit dome,
And stagger from stone to stone.

We were two, but yester-night;
And, faint, to this welcome sod
I have crawl'd, till he's out of sight –
And there's no one near, but God!
Cold, cold, cold:
And mine hour is nearly told!

When they come, for come they will,
Nor search this coast in vain,
They will find us sleeping still
On its lone unfriendly plain:
But none shall ever know
Till the great day comes, at last,
Our griefs in these realms of snow,
And the horrors of the Past!
For I sink on this fatal beach:
I have prayed with my latest breath:
And my struggles will only reach
The River of Life, in Death.
Cold, cold, icy cold:
And mine own last hour is told!

Edenhall Vicarage, Sept. 26, 1859   B. P.

Glossary

Words underlined are listed in the glossary in their own right.

Baleen: whalebone, sometimes also referred to as 'whalefins'.

Barque: a sailing ship with three masts where the aftermost mast carried no square sails. Some whaling ships were of this type.

Boat-steerer: the person responsible for steering the whaleboat while pursuing a whale.

Bomb vessel: bomb vessels were specially designed to mount heavy mortars (bombs) and required a solid bed on which the weapon could be seated. With the mortar removed and the bows strengthened with extra timbers the vessels could withstand the dangers of pack ice.

Bowhead whale (Balaena mysticetus): the whale hunted throughout the Northern Whale Fishery. The name 'Bowhead' was first given to *Balaena mysticetus* in England in the late nineteenth century. At the time of the whaling voyages described in this volume *Balaena mysticetus* was called the Right Whale or Greenland Right Whale.

Bounty: a payment initiated by the government in 1732 which had been designed to encourage the conversion of merchant ships into whalers. The rate varied depending upon the supply of whale oil. The payment finally ended in 1824.

Brig: a sailing ship with two square-rigged masts.

Bumpkin: a boom fixed to each side of the bow.

Clean: a whaling vessel that has returned without any whales.

Crew list: a list of information about a ship, its voyage and its crew kept as a result of the 1835 Merchant Shipping Act and filed with the Registrar Office of Merchant Seamen.

Dock: in inclement weather the crew were detailed to construct a dock in fast ice or an ice floe. This involved crew members standing on the ice with large ice saws and sawing a rectangular 'dock' into which the ship could be pulled in order to prevent her being squeezed by other floating ice.

Duck cloth: heavy plain woven cotton fabric commonly called canvas.

Fast ice: solid ice connected to the adjacent land. In contrast ice floes and pack ice are loose ice that moves according to wind and tide.

Fearnought: a heavy woollen cloth.

Fish: a whale

Fishing: the activity of catching whales was known as fishing.

Flensing/flinching: the activity of stripping blubber from the carcass of a whale while it was secured alongside the ship. The task was supervised by the spectioneer, and usually performed by the harpooners. The rest of the ship's company then packed the blubber into barrels which were loaded into the hold. The skeeman was in charge of this operation.

Flush decked: where the upper deck extends unbroken from bow to stern.

Greenlandman: a ship whaling in Greenland waters.

Head rails: the safety rail around the bow of a ship.

Hogshead: a liquid or dry measure, usually about fifty imperial gallons.

Ice floe: a sheet of floating ice.

Journalist: the name given to describe himself by the anonymous member of the ship's company who kept a journal aboard Skeffington Lutwidge's ship *Carcass*.

Kablunas: an Eskimo/Greenlandic word for 'white people'.

Land ice: ice that is attached to the shore and therefore does not move like pack ice.

Lead: a passage of open water through pack ice.

Line Manager: a skilled seaman responsible for coiling and arranging the lines that are attached to harpoons in the whaleboats.

Muster roll: a record of details of a ship, its voyage and its crewmen filed with the seamen's fund receivers on the arrival of a ship in port at the end of a voyage. Created by the 1747 Act for the Relief of Disabled Seamen. Muster rolls were superseded by crew lists resulting from the 1835 Merchant Shipping Act.

North Water: an area of year-round open water in the north of Baffin Bay.

Northern Whale Fishery: the name given to the Arctic whaling industry.

Pack ice: large areas of loose ice consisting of ice floes floating together. During the summer enormous quantities of pack ice float south down the east coast of Greenland.

Polynya: an area of sea that rarely freezes due to the action of currents such as North Water in Baffin Bay.

Puncheon: usually about 84 gallons of liquid.

Refraction: this refers to the peculiar property of light in the polar regions when ships, ice and icebergs can seem to be upside down above the horizon.

Rocknosing: a term to describe whale-ships working near land, often in uncharted waters where reefs were ever-present dangers.

GLOSSARY

Sawing: the process of sawing a passage through pack ice or land ice with ice saws.

Sea Horse: a walrus.

Ship: a sailing ship with three masts, square-rigged on each. Some whaling ships were of this type.

Skeeman: the crew member responsible for packing the blubber into barrels on board the whaling vessel. A skeeman is not always listed as a separate occupation in crew lists.

Snow: a type of brig.

Southern Whale Fishery: the name given to whaling in the South Atlantic and South Pacific. (Originally it referred to any whaling south of the Northern Whale Fishery.)

Spectioneer: the principal harpooner and man responsible for organising the flensing of a whale.

Squeezed: the term used when a ship is caught between two or more ice floes which drift together. This is an extremely dangerous event as the power and size of the floes can break the timbers of the ship and/or force the ship out of the water and onto the ice.

Tableaux vivants: in this context a group of native peoples arranged so as to demonstrate aspects of their everyday lives(eg. hunting, fishing).

Train oil: another term for whale oil.

Trophy: the name given to the display of stuffed creatures killed by a hunter.

Tun: a large cask of undefined measure but usually given as 252 gallons; according to Dr. William Scoresby a tun of whale oil weighed 17 cwts.

Umiak: a skin boat formerly used in the Arctic regions to carry people and their possessions to seasonal hunting grounds. They were often rowed by women and hence are sometimes referred to as 'women's boats'.

Unicorn: a narwhal.

Voyageurs: trappers and guides, often of French descent, active in the north of Canada.

Warping: the process of pulling a ship with ropes through a lead in the ice.

Whaleboat: an open boat about 25 feet long which was used to pursue a whale. Normally she had a crew of six, and a whaling ship carried six whaleboats. Each whaleboat was equipped with harpoons, lances and five lengths of whale lines consisting of 120 fathoms (720 feet) of 2½ inch hemp coiled in the bottom of the boat. These whaleboats could also be used to seek rescue if the whaling ship was wrecked.

Whalebone: the two rows of economically valuable baleen plates in the head of the Bowhead whale.